ONCE UPON A TIME THERE WAS (*MY*) TENNIS

Claudio
Pistolesi

ONCE UPON A TIME THERE WAS (*MY*) TENNIS

My Journey Through the Legends and Secrets of Tennis

Preface by
Adriano Panatta

Edited by
Sandra Eiko Tokunaga

GREMESE

Acknowledgments:
The Author wishes to express his special thanks to ATP Coach Weller Evans for his technical consultancy on the text of this project.

Cover: Francesco Partesano

Photo credits: Photos on the front cover and back cover by Angelo Tonelli. Photos on the cover, back cover and pp. 81 (bottom), 84, 85, 86, 87 and 88 were kindly provided by Ray Giubilo - Tennis Photographer.com. Other photos have been provided from the Author's personal archives. The Publisher has made all efforts possible to locate the names to be credited for all photos published in this book. If this has not been possible in all cases, please excuse any possible errors or omissions. The Publisher is prepared to complete any missing details in future editions of this book and is also prepared to recognize rights as per Article 70 of Law No. 633 of 1941.

Edited by: Sandra Eiko Tokunaga

Printed and bound by: Integrated Books International – Dulles, VA (USA)

ISBN 978-88-7301-796-7

Contents

Preface
by Adriano Panatta

Claudio Pistolesi's book (his first that is so strictly autobiographical) is irresistibly funny and at times sensational in the true stories it tells. Yet, it is also written with the profound passion of someone who truly loves and lives tennis. It is also an honest account of the often painful choices Claudio has had to make during his career and how he faced them.

I expected his book to be just like that because he is just like that—just like his writing, which you can read all in one breath. As a young man (that he was... and today as a former young man) with whom I share Rome as a birthplace and several unforgettable Davis Cup campaigns, Claudio has combined passion and courage with a thirst for a beautiful and exciting life. He has always liked being at the heart of memories created and adventures to be told.

Indeed, Claudio has certainly seen and experienced many things that deserve to be shared, whether over an after-dinner drink, during a party, or in a book... All together, these short but great stories take us into the universe of tennis and far beyond. The number of remarkable people Claudio has known in his life is astounding. Many have been his opponents, friends, and coaches... and there have also been unforgettable encounters during many decisive moments in his life.

I don't think there are many people like Claudio in today's world of tennis. He is someone who has successfully combined an impressive career on the court with a second career as a high-caliber coach, and a third, more mature one, as a representative of an entire profession. Today, it seems the coaching sector is rapidly developing and becoming ever more present on the circuit. Actually, to the extent where I wonder if it's truly necessary to have 1000 coaches for 500 tennis players...

To be clear, I am not questioning the teaching abilities of these coaches, or their usefulness, or even their ability to work well together in teams that resemble extended families. Indeed, almost all players have two coaches acting as heads of the household. Rather, I wonder if this situation risks compromising the ability of players, or students, especially if they are still very young, to act on their own. Will they be able to make the best choices in a match when these have not been prepared in advance?

I believe tennis players have a right to solitude, and this implies the right to risk making mistakes. However, I wonder if this is still possible today. Tennis players are constantly under escort. They are never left alone. In this respect, tennis has changed significantly. I already know that Claudio will want to give his ideas on these thoughts, and I will gladly listen. He is the one with first-hand experience as an instructor, and as an irreplaceable coach to legendary players such as Monica Seles, Davide Sanguinetti and Simone Bolelli. Claudio brought Simone to climb from No. 248 to No. 36 in the ATP rankings. He also led the top Japanese Davis Cup players and worked closely with Robin Söderling.

These are the names and faces that will guide you through a book you will want to read all at once. They will be joined by many other greats, from Connors to Federer, Wilander to Becker... and together, they will inevitably make you wonder: how on earth could tennis have thrived without someone like Claudio?

Introduction

For a long time now I have thought about writing something about my long adventure in the world of tennis. Now finally the time has come, and I am happy to welcome you to *ONCE UPON A TIME THERE WAS (MY) TENNIS*. Here I share with you the stories and anecdotes of my tennis career first as a player, and then as a coach – a profession I still pursue today and that gives me a sense of such great fulfillment.

Do not expect, however, a punctilious chronological review of events, with tournaments and scores lined up one after the other. This book is more like a long freewheeling narrative, or if you prefer, a long chat with friends. Here memories emerge on the thrust of the emotions that I experienced then, and that I now relive with you.

During my journey through tennis, I have been fortunate to have crossed paths with extraordinary champions. These great players, such as Adriano Panatta and so many others, have inspired and taught me such a lot. On the court, I won a lot, but I also faced incredibly difficult moments and hard-to-digest defeats.

I have travelled the world and come across a thousand different styles of play and sporting approaches. This became particularly true once I decided (thanks to Monica Seles) to stop competing and devote myself entirely to coaching. Over the years, I have been witness to all of the big and little transformations that international tennis has undergone, sometimes rejoicing in them, and sometimes not.

Sometimes I wonder how I have been able to keep going in tennis now for more than forty years. The only explanation is that as a child, at the Gianicolo Tennis Club in Rome, I developed a pure, visceral, and almost religious love for the sport of tennis. And I still find it intriguing to continue to explore tennis from all three hundred and sixty-degree angles, as a player, coach, journalist, and manager.

Here, with a generous scattering of the most fascinating, moving or crazy anecdotes from the world of tennis as I have lived it, is a condensation of my experiences in the pages you are about to read. I hope you will appreciate their spontaneity and honesty too. (Between you and me, I really couldn't have written the book any other way...)

Certainly, there are things in today's tennis that have changed since the '80s. This perhaps best explains the "(*MY*)" in the title. But one thing that has never changed is tennis' extraordinary ability to enthrall and enchant us always.

In the hope that these stories will leave you with an ever greater love for this unique sport. With thanks for joining me on this journey.

The Author

MY JOURNEY THROUGH THE LEGENDS AND SECRETS OF TENNIS

Preface by
Adriano Panatta

Caracas 1984

My maternal grandmother Enrica, whose last name was Cotogni, was the granddaughter of one of the greatest baritones of all time, Antonio Cotogni. He is remembered in the Rome quarter of Trastevere on a plaque that says: "The City of Rome to its favorite son". Grandmother Enrica had seven brothers and sisters. Two of them, Uncle Raffaele, known as Lello, and the other, Uncle Pietro, were two adventurers from another era. While participating in the campaign in Africa during World War II, they were taken prisoner by the British and were sent to a prisoner-of-war camp.

As a child I was fascinated listening to Grandma's stories about my great-uncles. To me it was like my father reading to me the adventures of Michael Strogoff or the Count of Monte Cristo. These great-uncles were like two heroes out of adventure novels to me. And the latest news was that they had moved to Venezuela, to Caracas... The family on my mother's side certainly had an adventurous, important, and very international history.

Caracas 1984

In 1984, one of the best years of my life, the Italian Tennis Federation was to decide who to send to compete in tournaments in North and South America at the end of the year.

The letter of invitation from the Federation arrived at home, a kind of conferral of title from the National Tennis Association, the highest institutional body. This was when we all still thought that state institutions were of the highest profile. I felt like Lancelot being knighted at the Round Table.

Grandmother Enrica, relying more on her Christian faith than on the international postal service, wrote to one of her two brothers, Lello. She sent her letter to an uncertain address that many years before had appeared on the last letter she had received from him. She had learned that the two brothers, in their seventies or so, were still alive and living in Caracas. She wrote to Lello that his 17-year-old grandson Claudio, as the Federation's letter announced, was to compete in an international tournament at the Italo-Venezuelan Club.

The rest happened as if we were in a movie... We arrived in Caracas with our coach, chaperone, and life educator, Gaetano Di Maso, a former national member of the Davis Cup team. We were taken to the luxurious neighborhood of Altamira, to a breathtaking hotel with an immense pool surrounded by lush greenery. The breakfast buffet, overflowing with fruit, pastries, and eggs cooked in every possible way, made me perceive South America as a land of abundance, sunshine, music and (I was seventeen) gorgeous girls...

Some doubt, however, began to cross my mind on the drive

from the hotel to the famous Italo-Venezuelan Club. I saw favelas, tin shacks along dirty waterways, with many sad-faced kids looking at our bus full of young tennis players. I couldn't quite put my finger on it then, but I sensed that tennis was definitely on the rich and privileged side of society, and this realization would stay with me for the rest of my life, right up to this day.

At the end of practice, I noticed a thin, noble-looking gentleman watching me. I was sweating and putting my rackets in my bag, but I stopped to take a good look at him. His face was somehow familiar. He said, "You are Claudio, aren't you? You have Enrica's eyes... it has to be you..." He spoke perfect Italian, but the underlying cadence of his Roman speech was unmistakable. Here in front of me was one of my two great-uncle adventurers... the protagonists of the novels of my childhood imagination that had taken me on travels to remote places all over the world.

I said nothing and went over to him. Tears welled up in my eyes, tears that I remember even today as I write and relive those moments. I looked at him and hugged him very tightly, still not knowing whether he was Piero or Lello, realizing that he was weeping with joy too. "Are you Uncle Lello or Uncle Pietro?" I finally asked. "I'm Uncle Lello – let's go for a ride, I have a car!" he told me proudly.

I realized that Gaetano, our coach, had witnessed the whole scene. As a true Neapolitan, of course, he could not have failed to instantly understand how special this occasion was. He felt he could make an exception and let me go with my uncle through the streets of Caracas, though he never would have normally, with his sense of responsibility.

The car was Uncle Lello's working tool. "I'm a driver for the Japanese". His tone was proud, the message was that he worked and was self-sufficient. "Claudio, always remember that the Japanese are serious, proper people who keep their word. If you get a chance, don't hesitate to work with them. I have a partner, Flora, who has a daughter, who is now my daughter," he added, a little afraid of saying so.

Knowing his sister Enrica, he was sure that she would not approve of a couple living together without being married. It did not sound very proper to me either, since that was how I had been brought up, yet deep inside I felt good about this new family, and it somehow made me happy. Many years later, I would also become a stepfather. I smiled at him, and he understood that not only did I not disapprove, but in fact I would be happy to meet them, and so, off we went.

Caracas was already a huge sprawling city. Uncle Lello, thanks to his job, knew it inside out. He showed me everything he could about the city along the way to his small, modest, well-kept apartment where everyone smiled and appreciated what they had. "How is Enrica? And your mom Giuliana?" he asked me, thirsting for news of all his relatives in Rome. Whenever I mentioned Rome to him, where he had not been for decades, he would suddenly have the sweetest smile.

I told him all about each of the Stampatori, Grandma Enrica's married name, and he rattled off stories of when they had grown up together, during the twenty years under fascism.

They had lived in a spectacular house opposite the Capitoline, though the house was unfortunately later torn down by Mussolini to make way for Via dei Fori Imperiali.

Uncle Lello also knew that at some point I would ask him an obvious question...

"Uncle? But your brother Pietro, Uncle Pietro, where is he?" I feared his answer. Instead, he said, "He lives not far from here, he has a garage. Do you want to meet him?" He said this thinking that if he didn't, his sister Enrica would never forgive him. He added, "You know Claudio, we haven't spoken for ten years, we had a fight and broke off forever".

Uncle Lello, however, took me about fifty meters from his brother's garage. I walked over. I saw a strong, older, dark-haired man working under a car. From underneath, he probably mistook me for someone else. "*Me pasas el gatto?*" he said to me in Spanish. A little confused, I thought he was talking about a kitten (in Italian *"gatto"* means cat), and I looked around, not knowing that in Spanish "cat" is a wrench.

"Uncle Pietro? Hi! I'm Claudio, Enrica's nephew". He came out from under the car and stared at me. He stood up, "You're Giuliana's son?" he asked in a broken voice. "Yes Uncle, I'm Claudio, Giuliana's son, and your sister Enrica's nephew". He hugged me tightly, and then stepped back with an expression of sheer disbelief and joy. He was smiling and very moved. Then he asked me, "But how did you find me, how did you get here?"

I turned and pointed to Uncle Lello, looking over at us from the car. They waved to each other, shyly. I took him by the hand and led him to Lello. "Hi Lello," "Hi Pietro," and all three of us hugged each other tightly, without saying a word. A miracle had taken place. Thanks to tennis, two brothers who had risked their lives together the world over, who together had left one continent for another, and who together shared the only link with their past, their carefully written letters to their sister Enrica, who was unaware of their quarrel, were reunited.

For the records, I made it to the final in the tournament, cheered on by the many Italian Venezuelans who had recreated a slice of 1950s Italy at their wonderful Club. I won the semi-final against Bruno Oresar, a Yugoslavian considered unbeatable among the players born in '67. Perhaps I got too complacent because of that victory, since I then lost in the final to an obnoxious player from Spain, against whom I should have won.

Uncle Lello, seeing me a little disappointed to have let him and the wonderful Italians in Caracas down, said "You did well, you made it to the final," perfectly reflecting the positive, happy attitude of the Stampatori. I returned to Rome and painstakingly recounted everything to Grandma Enrica. She listened to me, hanging on my every word and while smiling, she wept as she murmured, "This is a miracle from the Lord". Uncle Lello died of cancer a week after I returned to Rome.

This story just goes to show us how tennis can connect people, create excitement on and off the court, get us to write incredible stories about life, and make us travel. And travel is the university of life. In 1984 here were two brothers in Venezuela who had made peace after ten years thanks to a nephew who had come from Rome thanks to tennis. If that wasn't a miracle, it came close to it.

Boris the Great

Boris Becker was an absolute superstar in the '80s. In Munich when he went out for a walk, he stopped traffic. Boris loved the popularity and, unlike his main rival Stefan Edberg, did nothing to quell the fever. Years later he would unfortunately pay dearly for his love of attention and popularity.

Even with colleagues like us, he had this aura of superiority, though it was natural for him, and he didn't mean any harm by it. He was a torment to me though, as a personality and even physically, since he was a dozen centimeters taller and because though we were the same age, he had won a lot more matches since our Under-16 circuit period.

The ultimate spite, so to speak, was when Boris won Wimbledon in 1985, a magical year, and a year when we were both Juniors. But at the same time, I liked him very much, and he too was always affectionate and kind to me. He told me how important it had been to have shared all the Under-14 and Under-16 Juniors together. It was something he would remember for the rest of his life too.

Martin, my sports psychologist at the time, hoped to cure me of this inferiority complex I had when it came to Boris. Martin believed blindly in my potential, and according to him there was not a single reason why I could not beat Boris, especially on a clay court.

And the day came when, there on the Center Court of the wonderful tournament in Kitzbühel, Austria, Boris was waiting for me for our first match as professionals on clay. He was at the peak of his career. He was World No. 1.

Things were going well with the professor, my sports psychologist. I was among the first professional tennis players in history to receive sports psychological support from a professional in the field. I developed such a passion for the subject that many years later I majored in the study of Sports Psychology. I completed a degree in Science of Sports Coaching at an American university that had a Sports Psychology department.

"Claudio! Listen to me... the match against Becker starts long before the warm-up dribble. Every movement and attitude in the pre-match must be closely observed, absorbed, as emotional positioning that will be reflected on the court..." I had already lost to Becker four times, but I wanted to build on the defeats and this time in Kitzbühel I was determined to do better. "Look at what he does before the game, look at his face, and do what he does". The prof's message was clear to me. Show my formidable opponent that I was like him, and that nothing he did could intimidate me.

Boris had this way of looking at you with his eyes wide

open and his head tilted sideways. And I, counting on my natural talent as an imitator, for which I was well-known in the entire pro tennis world, in turn stared at him with the exact look. Becker surely must have thought that competitive anxiety had gotten the better of me that day...

We were taken by electric golf caddy to the wonderful Central Court in Kitzbühel, nestled in the Austrian Alps. It was a magical setting. In Kitzbühel, it feels as if you are living in a poem from Nordic mythology, where Siegfried could suddenly emerge at any moment.

The stadium was packed, with everyone there to watch the World No.1 play.

In the small gym where we were told to wait, I continued my psychological tactics. I had gotten off to a bad start because on the way to the stadium, Boris had put his bag right in the middle of my place. I didn't have the courage to ask him to move it, but tried to sit the best I could, perched on the very edge of the seat. It was a bad start. In the little gym, Boris was doing knee-high skips to warm up. I walked over to him and looked him in the face ... and I too started to get active and do the skip ... slavishly following the instructions of my sports psychologist.

Boris did not know whether to laugh or worry. He moved to a bench and used it to stretch his legs and do other stretches. I noticed that he had huge quads. I went next to him, threw a look at him, and did what he was doing. The imponderable in life is always just around the corner. My shoe was next to Becker's, the Diadora brand, like his, but marked "Boris Becker autograph..." I had my opponent's autograph on my shoe. I hadn't thought about that. He beamed at me – he knew he had already easily won the pre-game psychological challenge. "*Good shoe, right?*" he asked, and left me wondering what he meant.

I turned away and let it go.

But I made my real masterpiece bungle making my entrance into the Center Court. For this moment you are supposed to choose a piece of music to accompany your appearance.

Boris chose first. It was "The Eye of the Tiger," by Survivor, the music from *Rocky*. It was the best soundtrack for any athlete who grew up during the 70s and 80s. "The Eye of the Tiger" exhilarated the spectators, who greeted Becker's first steps as World No. 1 with a deafening roar.

Then it was my turn to make my entrance. The song I had chosen, caught up in a patriotic spirit, was a popular tune by Toto Cutugno, "The Italian". In Austria they have a very specific idea of Italians, that is, as being all pasta, religion, mom and guitar (or mandolin...).

The first words of the song, as many Italians will remember, went "*Buongiorno Italia... spaghetti al dente...*" and then, "*lasciatemi cantare, con la chitarra in mano, sono un Italiano*!" ("let me sing, as I play my guitar, I'm an Italian...". It was precisely the stereotype that Austrians and Germans have of us Italians. And the "Buongiorno... spaghetti al dente... chitarra" surpassed even the most obvious cliché.

Caught up in hysterical laughter, everyone began chanting these words repeatedly. They were shouting, partly because they were already a little tipsy from the afternoon beer, which was normal in those countries especially when on holiday, "*Buonciorno spaketti!*" mispronouncing it all and laughing uproariously. But for me, it was certainly not the best reception as I was announced onto the Center Court for a match against a Legend.

Anyway it was my own fault. Many years later I realized how this confirmed how an unnecessary and stupid reverential fear of foreigners had always held me back as a player. It was a cultural handicap. I don't know whether stemming from an exaggerated xenophilia or from something personal and ancestral that I had inherited from maybe even part of my family.

I lost 6-2, 6-2, but what disappointed me most of all about myself was my inability to handle negative emotions, my psychological subservience. Like all negative experiences as a player, discovering my own personality weaknesses became a powerful teaching tool as I pursued my professional life. The real wealth of a coach who has been a good tennis player is precisely the mistakes he made himself when on the court.

Two Years with the Legendary Monica Seles

In the mid-nineties I made the painful decision to end my career as a professional tennis player. I started working as a practice partner for Monica Seles, World No. 1. This was during her training period in Sarasota, Florida, in preparation for tournaments in Miami and Hilton Head, South Carolina. Sitting next to me in the players' box one day was a friendly bearded gentleman in his 40s who introduced himself as Paul, Monica's friend. He was eager to ask me a lot of questions about tennis, admitting that he didn't know much about the sport at all.

I hung out with him all week during that tournament. A couple of times as I watched Monica's match, I was lucky enough to already predict a double fault by her opponent as we talked. Paul was impressed. The day before the semifinals he came over during the warm-up session. "Claudio! I've got to go now. My NBA basketball team, The Portland Trail Blazers, is playing in New York tonight". and he gave me a hug. I thought he was an avid NBA basketball fan, and I immediately told him that my team was playing that night too. I was lucky, though, because I root for the Miami Heat, and they were playing in Miami.

A smile escaped his lips, “No, no, I own the Blazers”, he said offhandedly, adding, “but that’s not the team I root for”. From the way he was dressed, the simplicity of our encounter, the modest way he listened to all my explanations about tennis, I had never suspected that I had met Paul Allen, co-founder with Bill Gates of Microsoft...!

All that week, without even realizing it, I had been chitchatting and explaining tennis to the man who, at twenty-two, together with his friend Bill Gates, had left university in the mid-seventies and founded a little company, Microsoft (!). Their hope was to popularize the personal computer around the world. I had been travelling with my first PC laptop at the time, and I then recalled that just a few days earlier, being so proud of it, I had even shown it to Paul. I had asked him if he liked it, and if he happened to understand anything about computers. I even asked him if he might have an adapter for American plugs.

I was asking for an adapter for my computer from the founder of Microsoft... This was the owner of the “Octopus”, the world’s largest yacht. He was the fourth richest man on the planet according to the famous Forbes ranking, and a co-owner of DreamWorks with Steven Spielberg and Jeffrey Katzenberg. For several days, however, to me he had just been my new friend Paul. He genuinely liked me because he understood very well that I had no idea of who he was, or of his power or wealth. I don’t think that happened to him very often. I realized then how people whose success stories may have put them on top of the world still needed humanity, sincere relationships and friendship.

The campaign leading up to Roland Garros 1997 included tournaments in Rome and Madrid and then, before Roland Garros, a week of training somewhere in the South of France.

Monica was on a winning streak and was very happy. We had a dream location for practice, so spectacular it surpassed anything we could have imagined. A perfect clay tennis court had been built there especially for us, and we practiced assiduously. Paul Allen was also famous for throwing memorable parties with guests such as Sting, Geena Davis, who was my partner in mixed doubles just for fun. There was also Robin Williams, and Alan Rickman, the Sheriff of Nottingham in Kevin Costner's *Robin Hood*. And then there was Princess Leia from *Star Wars*, Carrie Fisher, and other equally famous stars.

Thanks to tennis, to which I will be indebted all my life, I was able to chat about art history with one of the finest actors in Hollywood, Robin Williams, and exchange a few words with all of these artists. It still moves me when I think about it. Art in all its forms has always been one of my greatest passions. The concentration of artistic talent around me in those days was phenomenal. I will be forever grateful to Monica and Paul for this as well.

After that we went to Paris. It was hard for me to dive back into the frenzy of booking practice courts (again eternally competing with Steffi Graf's team) and working like a maniac at returns (I was serving hundreds of times a day for her to practice returns in all possible directions and rotations).

The semi-final of that 1997 Roland Garros was unforgettable. Martina Hingis was now at her peak, but Monica was sure that with her experience she could beat her and make it very difficult for Hingis' umpteenth Grand Slam tournament. Hingis' mother was also her coach. Though in violation of the "no coaching" rule, she kept talking in her native Czech to her daughter from her box. She was doing this even though Martina was Swiss.

Giorgina Clark, historic supervisor and the charismatic chief of WTA was there. I pointed out to her that this was not allowed. I was very fond and appreciative of Monica, and I never liked to see injustice. I would have done what Hingis' mother was doing, but I would have been caught right away speaking in English. Many years later, as discussed further on in this book, I became the architect for the legalization of coaching during matches. This experience was one of my motivations.

In the end, Monica lost, and she was heartbroken. I wished I could have found the words in English at the time. The difficulty of language had been an obstacle in my work with Monica. Indeed if there is any precious advice I would like to give to teenagers who might be reading this book, it is to stress to them how important it is to make the effort right away to learn English fluently.

"One Moment in Time"
My Amazing 30th Birthday

The phenomenal singer Whitney Houston dedicated "One Moment in Time" to all the tennis players in attendance. They had all been U.S. Open winners. The event was the inauguration of the Arthur Ashe Stadium, New York, still the largest tennis stadium in the world. It was August 25, 1997, my 30th birthday. I told myself that "One Moment in Time", sung just a few steps away from me by Whitney Houston in person (who was a breathtakingly beautiful woman, by the way), definitely was an unforgettable birthday present.

Thanks to Monica Seles, with whom I had the privilege of working, we had full-fledged front row seats to that very special and unique evening. I recalled that years earlier when Monica had won the tournament, I had contributed as a practice player, at least a little, to her victory, ensuring that she was well trained every day. Monica was in game attire because when the concert was over, it would be her turn to open the first evening session in the history of Arthur Ashe Stadium. It was truly "One Moment in Time".

A week later, as Monica made her way quite smoothly through the tournament, she had Irina Spirlea as her opponent, a very fearsome Romanian player. I knew Irina well because she was the girlfriend (now wife) of a tennis player friend of mine from Rome, and especially because she and I had shared an important victory five years earlier in Jakarta, Indonesia. In 1992 in the Indonesian capital, I had talked a lot with Irina, who was friendly, intelligent and already spoke perfect Italian. We were both overjoyed to have won such an important tournament, with 100,000 dollars in prize money, at that time a big award.

One of the advantages of being a pro tennis player is that you come into direct contact with so many different cultures and countries. Fellow tennis players or others with whom you form friendships on the ATP and WTA circuits tell you their stories. In Romania only three years before I met Irina, there had been a revolution and the horrendous events in Timisoara. Irina grew up in a world where from the time she left for school in the morning, to the tennis center for practice in the afternoon, and then on her way home in the evening, she had to measure every word that even remotely sounded like criticism of the infamous dictator Ceausescu.

The "Securitate," a special militia of the fierce and brutal dictator, was not messing around. Our Romanian brothers and sisters had been under his rule for decades. The danger, Irina explained to me, was the risk of being denounced for a petty reward by spies who might well have been neighbors, schoolteachers, or tennis coaches. After the revolution, the Romanian youth of Irina's generation finally saw a glimmer of hope for a world of freedom and happiness. I thought of her Italian tennis peers at the time whose greatest concern at tournaments might be how precise a stringer was.

Irina's match against Monica in Arthur Ashe Stadium was very tight. Monica suffered from Irina's great serving power and forehand, and I was worried. Monica, with her usual indomitable courage, reached match point. This was very bravely saved by Irina, also with a bit of luck. Irina won, achieving that moment of pure happiness and, I am sure, fixing "One Moment in Time" forever in her life, just as Whitney Houston had sung to us a week earlier. Yet I was very sorry for Monica, whom I loved and still love dearly. I would have liked with all my heart to have seen her triumph again in New York, at the U.S. Open, where I had met her and won her trust a few years before.

Lady Diana on the Next Court

Like a recurring dream, the memory will never leave me of my weeks at the world's most important tournaments as a member of Monica Seles' team. During the 1997 Wimbledon tournament, off-court events were to impact my life even more so than on-court ones. There were long periods during which we could only wait for the inevitable London rain to stop. My new friend Paul Allen was a regular guest in Monica's box, and he and I kept each other company. Monica had met my sister Cinzia, who was part of our group, and there was a fourth guest, a familiar face, who sat behind me. He was Peter Gabriel of Genesis...

My sister was an impassioned musician, and when I introduced her to Peter, she was absolutely thrilled. We learned that the second-round match was cancelled. Monica's agent, young Tony Godsick (who so many years later would become the most famous agent of all as Roger Federer's business partner) quickly arranged a practice session at the Harbor Club. This was a luxurious country club in Chelsea where it was rumored even the British royal family would be seen.

Everything was impeccably organized, with Court 1 booked for Monica and I. It was a very fast synthetic surface and so great for simulating bounces on grass. We quickly headed for the locker rooms to change and, as we went in, a little boy slightly bumped into me. He looked up mortified, "*I am really sorry Sir...*" I thought to myself, "what an extremely polite little boy".

We began our ritual warm-up. Knowing Monica, I was sure we wouldn't be leaving the court for at least another two hours. It was about four in the afternoon. On the next court I glimpsed someone's figure. It was Pat Cash. I had played against him some ten years previously, in Melbourne in 1987, during the second round. It was the year he became Wimbledon champion. A few minutes later, I then noticed he was playing against a tall woman. She also played quite well, and I assumed she might be a friend of his whom he was tutoring. She, too, looked vaguely familiar.

During a break, Pat Cash came over to say hello to Monica and to greet me too (he had always shown great respect for me after our four-hour struggle at the Australian Open (he won by a whisper...). I then saw the woman he was with more clearly and recognized her. My heart skipped a beat. She came over and shook my hand, "I'm Diana, nice to meet you"... and I, overwhelmed and paralyzed with emotion, gratefully introduced myself as Claudio. And that was it. I saw that she, Lady Diana Spencer, appreciated the simplicity of our exchange of courtesies. Of course, in any case, with my origins as a boy from Rome's Via del Forte Bravetta, Monteverde district, this was the only way I knew how to be. Diana and Monica greeted each other warmly. Lady Diana had a sweetness and empathy that no one could imagine unless they had the opportunity of meeting her in person. For me, it was definitely one of the great honors of my life that I was fortunate to have had. As I went back to practice, I smiled to myself at the thought that the little boy who had accidentally bumped into me at the locker room door was William, the future King of England.

A month later we were in New York at the U.S. Open. It was August 31, 1997, the morning of one of Monica's matches. The shocking news reached us of Diana's death. We learned that she had been killed in a car accident in the Pont d'Alma tunnel in Paris, with her partner Dodi Al-Fayed. They were being chased by paparazzi who had been stalking her.

Monica was devastated and so was I. We could not say a word during our ride from Manhattan to Flushing Meadows. It was hard to concentrate during the match. Monica would never say so, and she would be angry if anyone did, but I honestly feel that the news heavily affected her performance in the tournament that year.

Jimmy Connors and His Poster

I walked onto the Center Court at the U.S. Open in Flushing Meadows to play against Connors. I couldn't help thinking that in my little room in my parents' house in Rome, Connors' poster was still on my wall. I cherished that poster. Connors had always represented the epitome of tennis to me ever since I was a child, along with Adriano Panatta, who was also present at that match as Italy's technical director.

It was 1986 and I had just turned nineteen. With the invaluable guidance of Paolo Bertolucci, my coach, I was thrilled on my debut to have qualified for what I considered the most important tournament of all, the U.S. Open. In the Majors, or Grand Slam tournaments as they are also commonly called, with 128-player fields, today the seeds are 32. This was a change that took place in the early 2000s. Previously there were only 16 seeded players.

I was not happy to see that in the first round I had been drawn to play against Ulf Stenlund, World No. 22. As I studied the big scoreboard, my gaze fell on the next name that, if I won, I would play against in the second round. It was indeed him – Jimmy Connors! He was the player I had watched most keenly on TV as a youngster, hoping to learn from him. After Connors' Wimbledon final against Borg in 1977, lost in the fifth set, I went to the garage (I was ten years old) and against the wall I replayed the same final, imitating a shot each from Borg and Connors, to make Connors win. A chill ran down my spine at the mere thought that now I had the opportunity of playing for real against Connors.

Despite the ranking difference, I won against Stenlund in three sets, and already a second after winning match point against Stenlund, I was mind and heart on the Center Court. The Louis Armstrong stadium with a capacity of 14,000 seats was always packed and there I was to challenge the immortal Jimmy Connors. Rino Tommasi did an on-court interview of me for TV Capodistria. At the time this was the ultimate in free-to-air tennis modernity. It broadcast a commentary of the match the next day that I still have today, with Gianni Clerici pointing out rather proudly that there was a 19-year-old Italian on the Flushing Meadows Center Court.

Two days later I was in the locker room next to Connors who was laughing and joking with everyone. I was sitting in a corner with my yellow Walkman and listening to Madonna. Then they called the match and as I heard over the loudspeaker "*Mr. Connors... Mr. Pistolesi... Please go to the Center Court...*"

I truly wondered whether I was dreaming or if it was all for real.

The security people led the way, opening a passage for us through the wall of fans cheering Jimmy and trying to touch him. The wall closed up again before I could get through and I had to elbow my way through the three hundred meters that separated the locker room from the Central, even taking insults from people who could not have imagined that I was Connors' opponent.

My coach Paolo Bertolucci had prepared me very well for the match and I kept repeating his words in my mind to reassure myself. Being a tennis history buff, I remembered that in 1978, only eight years previously, Adriano Panatta had challenged Connors on that very court. He had lost in five sets in a spectacular, historic match. I thought that I absolutely had to be up to representing Italy again, with dignity, in exactly the same situation.

The stands rose steeply and the roar was deafening on that beautiful sunny day. It was very hot and muggy. I kept my eyes to the ground so as not to be intimidated by the thousands of spectators. But I was happy, I couldn't have been happier just to be there, a week after my 19th birthday. I was relying on my confirmed mobility skills and my forehand, which it was said was unrivaled, even against Connors.

The match began well for me. My high flailing forehand was going into his left-handed forehand at shoulder height which was very uncomfortable for him. I was later told that John Newcombe, doing the commentary for American television, had said that I very wisely never went to the net, so as not to expose myself to Connors' deadly passing shots. Even less did

I try to serve and volley, which would be meaningless against the best returners of all time. The truth was that I didn't feel confident at all in the net game, and I never went there against any opponent. It wasn't a choice for that particular moment. But unintentionally it looked great as a tactical choice.

I was practically flying on the court, spinning my forehand and giving Connors a hard time. Rino Tommasi and Gianni Clerici were excited, overcome by a mixture of joy and astonishment as they called the match. In the first set it came down to a tie-break. Some of the line judges' calls were really unfair, and, perhaps encouraged by my Roman, somewhat Gascon spirit, I dared to complain to the chair umpire. He, like all the umpires, was intimidated by the great Connors. I remember my lips could be read clearly, and my words did not escape Gianni Clerici, when I said verbatim on the U.S. Open Center, *"Li mortacci vostri"* to the umpires. Fortunately, no one understood.

"He 'punched' Connors!" said Clerici. *"Pugnetto"* is an Italian tennis expression for making a fist in the direction of an opponent. It is a gesture of personal challenge on the court, not sanctionable but considered quite provocative. I was in the match, and I could tell that my childhood idol was very annoyed that an Italian kid who came from the qualifiers was facing him in such a brazen way. And he made some strong gestures to rebuke me.

Pancho Segura was in his corner. He was a mythical figure of '50s and '60s tennis (bigger than Pietrangeli, just to give you an idea). I knew everything about him, having memorized the best book ever written on tennis, *500 Years of Tennis,* edited by Gianni Clerici. This was the very Clerici who was now doing the commentary. Adriano Panatta was sitting next to my coach, Paolo Bertolucci, only eight years after his match with Jimbo, and next to him was Clarissa Burt, one of the actresses I most admired, cheering me on.

At that match there was an incredible tornado of emotions and memories crisscrossing with figures that were almost myths to me. They put me in such a euphoric state that I had a real chance of beating Jimmy Connors at Flushing Meadows. In the tie-break of the first set a serve from my opponent ended up two inches out. I was on the ball but stopped to prepare for the second serve. Silence from the umpires.

From then on, I sensed that one way or another, Jimmy had to move on in the tournament. For goodness' sake, it would have been a titanic feat if I did win, yet everyone there, including myself, felt I had a chance. Unfortunately, it would not be until twenty-five years later that they would invent the "Hawk Eye," the electronic live call. The match ended after more than three hours. I lost 7-6, 6-3, 7-5, but at least I had the satisfaction of seeing Connors an absolute wreck.

I went back to the locker room proud of my game. In many ways for me it had almost been a victory, given the circumstances. Above all I was certain that I had represented Italy well on one of the most important courts in the world, and against one of the greatest champions of all time.

Melbourne 1987 at the Legendary Kooyong Lawn Tennis Club Facility

My first trip to the Australian continent was a marvelous adventure. Accompanied by my coach Paolo Bertolucci, at the time newly assigned to me by the Federation, we launched into the challenging task of learning to play on grass. This surface, compared to clay, demanded neuromotor capacities so distant from what we were accustomed to that it felt almost like you were playing a completely different sport.

The advantage of having a famous former tennis player as a coach is having access to other champions' coaching too. As soon as we arrived at the Adelaide tournament, Paolo asked Steve Denton, his friend who was a two-time finalist at the Australian Open, to coach with me. I found it very instructive to learn that I could expect each point to usually last only three shots at the most on grass.

Although the first round, on an outside court, was not one of the most important matches on the daily schedule, it held the great prospect of most likely going against Pat Cash in the second round on the Center Court. This was an extraordinary opportunity. My opponent, Michael Robertson from South Africa, was a specialist on grass. I relied on my serve, that with Paolo's help I had honed for that type of surface. What was more, I was in top condition.

In the first game of the match, I noticed Pat Cash's coach sitting in a corner of the grandstand. He was alone, with his arms crossed, and apparently studying his player's opponent. He was Tony Roche, a pillar of tennis history. Roche was said to have had the best backhand volley of all time. And as a coach, his players would go on to win many Grand Slam tournaments when his tremendous knowledge of the sport made all the difference. Roche coached champions such as Ivan Lendl, Pat Rafter and, most notably, Roger Federer. And he was looking at me – I summoned up all my strength and was determined more than ever to make all the right choices. It was almost as if I wanted to impress Tony Roche even more than win the match. But it worked. I won 11-9 in the fifth set, after four and a half hours, and Roche's sincere compliments will remain an indelible memory all my life.

Very few people know that I played at the Australian Open in Melbourne against Patrick Cash in January 1987. This was at the mythic Kooyong Lawn Tennis Club, home of the Australian Open until precisely 1987. It was where every tennis player who had trodden that grass was an immortalized champion (in one way or another). The second round of the tournament was lost in four sets by the local hero Pat Cash in a match that lasted three and a half hours

Cash even smashed a racket when he lost the second set because at that point he felt he was in such danger of losing the whole match. His blade-sharp volleys on his home grass were not so effective. The heat of the Australian summer had dried out the grass which was now more yellow than green, and the bounces became higher and more comfortable for a baseline hitter like me.

That year in July, Cash would go on to win the Wimbledon tournament. I lost the match, yet on Channel 7, Australia's main channel, broadcast live, I earned the respect and esteem of Australians, a quintessentially mature tennis people, and of Pat Cash himself. And still today, he honors me with his friendship. As mentioned, it was Pat, for example, who introduced me to Lady Diana Spencer, who was a friend of his. When I think about it, I still get the chills.

Let me explain about my comment previously that few are aware of my prestigious match in Melbourne. After all, I had just turned nineteen and there I was on one of the world's historic courts. Yet no significant trace of this remains. I recalled this fact only last year with Cash himself. We agreed that if at the time there had been the mass means for the promotion of tennis as exist today, the value of that match – more for me of course than for him – would have been blown all out of proportion.

Nowadays we are often stifled by the overwhelming ocean of information, videos and free commentary available on the Internet and social networks. Yet we can appreciate the importance that each tennis player receives from virtually global 24/7 exposure. Dedicated channels like Tennis Channel in the U.S. and Super Tennis in Italy give value to tennis players and help them in their bargaining power with sponsors, not to mention the personal satisfaction players enjoy from this exposure.

I wish I had had Super Tennis for that match with Pat Cash, I must admit. But it ended up that instead I was esteemed by the Australian public (and I am proud of the prestige this brought to tennis in Italy) but not in my own country. Many years later Super Tennis violently attacked me, and this I cannot forget, but that is another story that I don't feel like bringing up now.

Nevertheless, the Italian Federation Tennis channel deserves credit for having brought great international tennis to Italian fans, especially to the benefit of Italian tennis players. This has not only offered younger players an educational tool, but it has also given great exposure to established tennis players before public and sponsors.

The Victory Over Mats Wilander in Monte Carlo

In 1988, on Rome's birthday which is on April 21, the Italian news program TG1 went on the air ten minutes late. Giampiero Galeazzi was a pillar of the RAI Italian TV network, and his sphere of influence went way beyond sports. On that day he successfully managed to hold up the daily news program so that he could finish his commentary of Round 16 of the Monte Carlo tournament. Indeed, the World No. 1 was succumbing to a young Italian in his twenties, Claudio Pistolesi from Rome.

Mats Wilander was No. 1 in 1988. He had won the Australian Open and made it quite clear that he was the strongest player of the season. He overtook Ivan Lendl to become the top player in world tennis. Wilander won Roland Garros and the U.S. Open in the famous overtaking final against Lendl. To me, however, caught up in the magic of tennis in Monte Carlo, it did not seem at all impossible to beat him.

My tournament had started from the qualifiers. I won against Massimo Cierro, who was never easy to beat. It was me calling the shots with him that day and it was amazing how a change in playing conditions from the previous tournament in Madrid could have such an impact on my level of play.

In Madrid you play at about 500 meters above sea level, and it is always windy. In Monaco you play practically right on the sea in the most beautiful country club in the world. There, sunshine and clear windless days seem to have been agreed by contract. I also went on to win against the Australian Wally Masur, who later in his career reached the semifinals of the U.S. Open.

I had begun to truly apply the advice of my coach, Antonio Zugarelli, known as Tonino. The Italian Federation had surprisingly granted my request for him to coach me. Tonino was a great champion. Not too many years earlier, in ‘76, he had won the Davis Cup with the famous legendary “La Squadra” in Santiago, Chile.

He had quit playing a few years before he began coaching me and had seemed all but forgotten by high-level tennis. I had asked if he could be hired since I did not have the resources to do this privately. I was granted my request thanks to an enlightened and passionate manager, Chiarino Cimurri, another great man who unfortunately was taken from us all too soon.

My progress on the scoreboard continued by beating World No. 25, Peter Lundgren. The next day, I was playing a formidable game that leveraged my famous forehand. I had finally figured out how to put it to good use by following it to the net. It only took me two sets to eliminate Aaron Krickstein, an American who was always used as an example of how, according to the usual detractors, "They don't even play junior tournaments in America". This was to insinuate that my Junior World Champion title won three years earlier was not all that valuable. They remarked, "If you get a guy like Krickstein, who was already in the Top 10 at seventeen, it will only take a few games".

I received very special satisfaction from the words of Nicola Pietrangeli, a mythic figure of Italian tennis. He told the newspapers, referring to me, "You won't find any better tennis playing than that". In fact, if I had to choose the match in which in my entire career I raised my level of play to the highest, it would be that match with Krickstein. In addition, it opened the doors for me to the most panoramic and spectacular court in the world... the Monte Carlo Center Court. There I took on that year's World No. 1, Mats Wilander. I noticed that Boris Becker, my other peer, lost that day to my friend Marian Vajda, who became one of the greatest coaches in history. He was also the architect of Novak Djokovic's victories.

I went to see Ivan Lendl's matches, Yannick Noah's, Henri Leconte's, and Andres Gomez's. I remembered how many times as a spectator at the Foro Italico in Rome I had watched those very champions. Yet that day I was already a round ahead of them in a big tournament. My friends of my age had already lost. They had been above me in the rankings, players like Muster, Canè, Kent Carlsson, Perez Roldan, Mancini, and Skoff.

That morning at 11:00 on April 21, 1988, Giampiero Galeazzi was ready in the commentator's booth and I learned later that quite a lot of kids had skipped school to watch me play. During the warm-up moments of my life suddenly came back to me. All of the times my mom would pick me up from high school and bring a sandwich that I could have to not waste any time. I was tense and stiff now, but at the same time, I felt I had Mats Wilander within reach, with my forehand.

A few too many errors, a few good passes from him, and I found myself down 6-2, 3-1. Giampiero's commentary, accompanied by Roberto Lombardi, was like an obituary. "Pistolesi is taking a sound lesson from the Swedish champion, definitely out of reach for him". At that point came the so-called "flow", that "flow" of a state of grace. It is one that might only come a few times ever to some top-level athletes. It is very difficult to describe. Spatial-temporal perceptions change. Your breath is freed, and your body finds a perfect balance between relaxation and speed.

I remember word for word what I had said to myself at that moment. "If you stay calm, you can still win this set, forget everything else and just try to take back this second set, then in the third *you kill it!*" Point by point, I changed the inertia of the match, but not only because of my forehand. I was going to the net with consistency, opening up the court much better before the downswing, with the serve that was giving me so many free points. Giampiero Galeazzi was getting excited. From "Pistolesi" I was now becoming "our Claudio..."

The tie-break of the second set was dramatic. At 5-4 for me I hit the band of the net and lost the point through sheer bad luck. On the next point I played a short backhand ball and followed it to the net, Adriano Panatta style, and closed with a cross court volley.

The stadium was packed and now delirious. The spectators were surprised and fascinated by the spectacular game I was playing. Mats was visibly unnerved to have to go to the third set in a match that he thought he had already won. In the third I was in control of the game. At 5-2 to me, theoretically RAI 1 was to air the ritual newscast. RAI exceptionally decided to make it wait ten minutes. In life, thanks to my tennis, I postponed Italy's RAI news.

I won 6-2 without giving my opponent a chance to come back. The flow fortunately lasted until the end. On match point, when Wilander missed a backhand volley, I was so in shock with joy that I didn't even react. "Pistolesi strangely cool," Giampiero said, "he is not jubilant and is going over to shake hands with his opponent".

Tonino Zugarelli came down on the court, in tears, and we did a French TV interview together. I knew French and was amazed that he also responded perfectly in French, "Toni'! But when did you learn French?!" I asked him, and he said, "Never, but I'm so happy that now it's easy!" and down we went together in a liberating laugh mixed with tears. We both knew that we had just accomplished a feat that all the tennis fans of Italy, and beyond, would remember with tremendous joy.

“Vilas! Vilas!”

Roland Garros has an emotional impact on tennis fans like no other tournament. The moments in the ‘30s that went down in tennis history thanks to the “Quatre Mousquetaires” (the four French players Brugnon, Borotra, Cochet and Lacoste) are immortal. They have bestowed upon the wonderful Bois de Boulogne facility a wealth of tradition and importance that I would say are just as immortal. And this can be felt even by younger people today, almost a hundred years later.

One famous and indeed immortal year that everyone remembers was definitely 1989. And as it happened, not only was I there, but during that year I made it to the third round of the tournament. When the draw came out, my heart skipped a beat. I would be playing with another childhood idol of mine, the ‘poet of tennis’, Guillermo Vilas. He was the player who had opposed Adriano Panatta in the Final at the Foro Italico in 1976. I was there in the stands then, at nine years old, shouting my head off to cheer on the great Panatta.

As a boy, Vilas's poster was among my most coveted. It is still up on the wall in my childhood bedroom at my parents' house, in a prominent place next to Connors'. I was destined to play against Connors in 1986. And this time I was playing against Vilas!

He was a Vilas perhaps worn somewhat by his thirty-six years, but in big tournaments, perception and emotional balance change a lot. I would have to greatly raise the level of my play to win. Indeed, many years later, Nadal and Djokovic made us realize that at age thirty-six, Roland Garros could still be won. And not so many years earlier, Guillermo had made it to the final against Wilander.

We were assigned the court that definitely had the most atmosphere, a little jewel named after Philippe Chatrier. This was in tribute to the great longstanding President of the French Federation, and President of the International Federation. The warm-up evoked in my mind all of the times I had admired Vilas as the ultimate tennis champion. I vividly remembered the historic final that Vilas lost at the Foro Italico against Adriano, and then his victory at Roland Garros in 1977, and... in a moment... I was about to start a match against him at Roland Garros itself, and it wasn't all a dream...

As often happened to me when I found myself in the limelight, as that day in the jam-packed stadium, the level of my play began to soar. My service return was very long and consistent. I was in no hurry to accelerate my shots and, most importantly, I was "reading" the match from the beginning very well. Guillermo Vilas' heavy balls had lost a good thirty percent of their force. They had been one of his strengths. He was moving laterally with one less step than the phenomenal runner the whole world had seen climb the world rankings.

Incidentally, a word here if I may, of my opinion concerning the fierce controversy that still rages today between ATP and Vilas and his supporters, including prominent Argentine lawyers and journalists. This concerns the fact that in 1977, simply because of some technical data glitch (imagine computers in 1977) Vilas was not granted World No. 1 status. It would of course be ridiculous to compare the performance level of technology forty-six years ago with today's. Moreover, I think that just simple common sense makes it blatantly obvious that here is a tennis player who won sixteen tournaments, including three Grand Slams, all except Wimbledon, where he still made it to the quarters.

I was thinking about the many pages of tennis history that had been written by my opponent, as I was beating him on the court. And the more I thought about it, the more my level of play rose, as if I too were making history. I was stronger than Vilas that day, and with uncanny serenity I brought home the first two sets and got to match point in the third. All hell broke loose in the stands. It was as if the Parisian audience did not want to let go of one of its most beloved champions. And, paradoxically, neither did I!

A chorus rose up, urgently chanting the two syllables of Vilas' last name, as sharply as one of his backhand passers. "Vi-Las Vi-Las..." and more and more people joined in, moved by the chanting. The referee timidly tried to stop the chorus – "*S'il vous plait*" – but this only put more fuel on the fire. The chanting rose even louder and I had the distinct impression that the whole facility had joined in, and not just the spectators of the court Philippe Chatrier.

It was my spontaneous reaction to simply lay my racket down on the ground. And in my immense affection for Guillermo, truly, I too joined the chanting. This was even despite the fact that I was his opponent, and that the match was still in progress. He saw me and smiled gratefully. We played the last point, and not even for a moment did the chorus subside. I won the game, and the hug I exchanged with Guillermo Vilas, both of us in tears, will remain in my heart forever.

He felt my peace and admiration for a great champion. He had been the example I had grown up with as a youngster. It had contributed to my becoming a professional tennis player myself. And in all the years that followed, whenever we happened to see each other, he greeted me with obvious affection, and this special affection was mutual.

Me and the Davis Cup with Adriano Panatta as Captain

My first invitation to the Davis Cup, the greatest dream any child who played tennis in the '70s could have had, came in 1986. I was eighteen, and the Captain who summoned me was Adriano Panatta, Yes, *the* Adriano Panatta. My teammates were Gianni Ocleppo, who though nearing the end of his career, was still a very good doubles player; Francesco Cancellotti, a champion whether on or off the court, as well as being my model of playing based on a very strong forehand like mine; and Claudio Panatta, Adriano's brother, ten years his junior, and who was also a very close friend of mine.

We used to play in Palermo, a city I came to know and love very much. This was at the historic clubhouse of the Favorita, under the picturesque Monte Pellegrino. Even in February, it was warm and sunny as we trained in Mondello, or as we had lunch outdoors at the National team's hotel, the Villa Igea (Palermo's most famous hotel), overlooking the sea. Ten years later Villa Igea became famous and popular all over Italy thanks to Roberto Benigni who chose it as a location for his film *Johnny Stecchino*.

I was the reserve player, but I was on the national team, wearing the Blue Jersey, my very first one, that I have kept to this day. I hadn't even turned nineteen yet. This Blue Jersey would be followed by many more. I liked the thought that Blue Jerseys had been worn by the great Italian tennis players of the '70s. And that among them, even beyond my greatest, most extraordinary childhood dreams, Adriano Panatta, who was now my captain. The Blue Jersey had been worn by Pietro Mennea, Paolo Rossi, Dino Meneghin, and the Abbagnale brothers. And the list of the great Blue athletes of the '80s, who had always marked my life in sports, grew longer every time I lost myself in these thoughts.

We then received the invitation that took us to Seoul, South Korea. It was a country that at the time we knew very little about, but that would organize the Olympics only a year later, in 1988. Claudio Panatta was still with me. He was a very strong player who had to bear the enormous burden of having Panatta as his surname, with his legendary brother on the bench. It always seemed to me that Adriano was extremely demanding of his little brother. But you could tell how much he loved Claudio and wanted to stimulate him to aim for higher and higher goals. Indeed, for Adriano it was not an easy situation to handle.

In the evenings, Adriano got busy in the kitchen. Armed with pots and pans and ingredients brought from Italy, he cooked us the most extraordinary pastas. During those weeks together I think I truly discovered Adriano, the person, apart from the iconic image of the historic tennis athlete. Adriano was generous and he was pleased that others were too. He was also shy and modest when talking about his triumphs. In fact, I have always been struck by the fact that he does not even know where his trophies are, not even those from his victories at the tournaments at Roland Garros or Foro Italico.

He enjoys the good things in life, without a doubt, but always with enormous respect for others. I think that out of necessity, he built a shell around himself, a gruffness that was always ready to desecrate anything that did not respect his codes of life. There was a video that went viral on social media in which Adriano is at the airport and is interviewed by a young man who had not recognized the great tennis champion. Adriano's responses as he explains the beauty of tennis to the young interviewer are not only hilarious but absolutely brilliant.

The Davis match against South Korea was tough. Claudio Panatta lost after a five-hour struggle against an opponent who, though he did not play on the international circuit, was quite a legend in Asia. He was extremely powerful and athletic. Claudio, taken by surprise, came out of the defeat devastated.

The elite of Italian tennis journalism were always following in our wake. Above all there was Rino Tommasi who, unlike today, seemed happy in those days to explain to the tennis world why in their opinion we were "mediocre" players. This was their favorite adjective, and they found themselves in trouble when, instead, we often delivered high-level performances.

Paolo Canè courageously settled the dispute by winning the decisive match with the tie at two all. This decisive match was played on Tuesday because of the incessant rain. Military helicopters were used on the Center Court of the Olympic tennis stadium to blow the court dry.

During six wonderful years, my life revolved completely around those invitations to play on the Davis Cup team, the National Tennis Team. I remember very clearly the most beautiful moment of all. In Bari, to me a magical tennis city, Adriano Panatta called me over to a room at the Circolo Tennis. He told me that he was confident that I should play as a starter. It was a very delicate match, against Denmark. This match was decisive for Italy to remain in the elite echelons of world tennis, the so-called "World Group". Italy, in case of defeat, would suffer the humiliation of being eliminated for the first time. A historic relegation to the B series in short.

Adriano Panatta had personally decided to entrust me with the tennis defense of our country, to maintain a dignified presence among the other great tennis powers of 1991. We were stronger than them, but at Davis you never knew. The other starter, an indispensable player, was my great friend Omar Camporese. From '90 to '92 he had won a place for himself as one of the strongest players in the world.

What I recall of the day we played that match, in September when the temperature in Bari was still above 30 degrees Celsius, was breakfast. Omar had made himself a nice hot chocolate, which he always loved instead of coffee... "But are you sure? In this heat..." I said. It was no problem, he assured me. Yet during his first match, against the tough Dane, Frederic Fetterlein, his stomach started acting up all right. And he lost.

Omar is such a sweet, sensitive and generous person. In the locker room, consumed by guilt, he broke down in tears. At that moment it was as if life was asking me to muster up all the courage and inner strength I could to accomplish this mission, whatever it took to win. Indeed, mathematically, at that point, if I did not win at least one match, I was destined to go down in history as the player who had sent Italy, for the first time, to second division.

Without a second thought, I went over to Omar. I took his head in my hands and looked deeply into his eyes. “Look Omar I’m going to win three sets to love now and then tomorrow we’re going to beat these Danes!” I blurted this out, instinctively, and Adriano heard my words and his eyes approved. Adriano Panatta was my most precious accomplice during that time, one of the hardest, most intense moments of my life.

My opponent, Michael Tauson, who was almost two meters tall, had a great serve. I was very impressed by his Davis victory over Stefan Edberg, albeit one that took place at home, in an indoor arena with a very fast court. Playing on clay was to my advantage.

The team presentation ceremony, my first as a starter, was held between the first and second matches of the day. I found myself standing in line and at attention, next to Adriano. He was a bit nervous but still conveyed unconditional confidence in me. Nothing could have made me happier or prouder than this trust. The notes of Mameli's anthem struck up. As a history buff, I remembered all the words of our national anthem, even those of the second part, which not many people know by heart.

Life was putting me before an important test. I had to bring out the best in myself, play my most solid game, and beat this Tauson no ifs or buts. I was so charged up that tears began streaming down my face, not out of sentiment, but out of pure competitive rage. I couldn't wait to start grinding out my victory, thanks to my forehand.

This was my national debut, a match of three sets to five which differed so greatly from regular tournaments. Yet I had Adriano Panatta on the bench, in tennis history one of the most experienced professionals to have faced similar situations. I won the first two sets 6-0, 6-1. And Adriano, I could feel, was immensely pleased with me. It was perhaps the happiest moment of my whole career. The third set got complicated. I was perhaps too confident that I had already won, and I lost a few too many points out of haste. But then in the tie-break of the third set, despite some nervous cramping in my right hand, I regained control of the situation, and won.

With relief in my heart beyond words. And then came the affectionate long hug with my childhood idol – Adriano Panatta, my captain. We then went on to win the doubles. Omar Camporese, also so grateful to me for having saved the day, won on the third day, ending the match for good to the delight of the stadium packed with Italian fans who had come to Bari to cheer us on.

Many years later, in the wonderful medieval village of Bettona, during an international coaching course organized with the ATP, I had the privilege of spending the entire day with Adriano. He told me things about himself that although we had spent many years together, I did not know. Few people ever wondered how it was possible that the most important champion of Italian tennis, from a country traditionally of clay courts, was known in the world for his net game. "Because he was talented" is the offhanded rather uneducated explanation we most often hear.

I learned from Adriano himself that his mentor, the great Mario Belardinelli, had suggested to Adriano, who was 20 at the time, to go to Australia to train. There, Adriano became part of the group of great tennis players in that country. In Australia, they played exclusively on grass. In the late '60s, three out of four Grand Slam tournaments were played, precisely, on grass. The foresight and tennis culture of Mario Belardinelli, the architect of Italian tennis success during those years, was impressive.

Adriano talked to me about Lew Hoad, a legendary Australian champion. He was considered by many even better than Rod Laver. Hoad took Adriano under his wing and they played every day. That experience taught Adriano, as he puts it, the "geometry" of the tennis court. He learned the best possible way to cover the net after an approach, or after a followed forward serve.

Adriano stayed in Australia for six months. This was at a time when means of communication were not very developed. He spent this period with a group of tennis players who were not only absolute world-class, but who were also in formidable athletic condition. They were coached by the great Harry Hopman, the daddy of all coaches in the world.

Hopman had made physical culture for tennis players his credo. Adriano Panatta worked intensively and diligently to get to the top. He returned to Italy to train in Formia with Mario Belardinelli, an equal to Hopman in tennis culture. Adriano continued working out in the same place where, for example, another legendary champion dear to Italians had his base, although in another sport, Pietro Mennea. Adriano kept up this exhausting training for years, both on the court and in the gym, and it was bound to lead to a career like his. The unjust claim that Adriano Panatta was a lazy, apathetic athlete who shunned training, is totally untrue.

As Adriano continued reminiscing to me, I recalled his advice from the Davis bench during my matches. I may not have fully understood everything then. Indeed, I never did have a good foundation for net games, my strength being in other areas of the court. But in retrospect I can truly appreciate the tremendous value of those detailed tennis arguments by our greatest champion. He was definitely one of the most knowledgeable in the world. If I had it all to do over again, I would try to spend much more time with him.

"Hoad had told me that I was going to win Wimbledon, even more than once," Adriano continued, "and I felt that in '79 everything was ready for that to happen. I sensed the truth of that moment". As Adriano had often stated, his greatest regret was the 1979 edition of Wimbledon. He lost a match that he was supposedly sure to win. This was against a certain Pat Dupré, an American player at least two classes lower than Adriano.

Although in tennis there are no "ifs", in the semifinals he would have played against Roscoe Tanner. Adriano had never lost against him. In the finals, he would have challenged Bjorn Borg, whom he had beaten very often. "I used to win against Bjorg because when I brought him to the net, he was just a wimp," he told me.

Just then, I understood the greatness of a champion. Words like that by anyone else might have sounded like stratospheric arrogance, but from Adriano Panatta they were the absolute honest truth. When it came to touch and tennis "fencing," where the ball is very low and slow, and where physical power is not important, Adriano was a master compared to the Swedish champion. In my opinion, Borg was very lucky not to have found himself facing Adriano in the final at Wimbledon in 1979.

Adriano explained to me how he had been surprisingly eliminated from the tournament in the quarterfinals. Pat Dupré, an American tennis player of average stature, had been the designated victim for the day to play against the great Adriano Panatta. The match, as expected, ran smoothly in favor of our great tennis player. Then, somewhat almost bored, Adriano started joking with the spectators, and conceded a few strokes, more for show than for the competition. He became distracted, as can happen in our sport, and the match changed direction.

Dupré felt he had been given a chance and began to play at a level he had never attained in his life before. Adriano, perhaps blaming himself for not having finished the match sooner, became tense and made mistakes... and lost. His greatest regret in so many years of an extraordinary career was that very match. He was recalling all of this to me over lunch, with such humility and shyness. I could not believe the enormous privilege I had that Adriano Panatta, my boyhood idol and national team captain, was confiding in me as he relived these emotions. I was so very moved.

I realize that the picture I have painted of Adriano, that is, of someone who was hardworking, humble, generous, sensitive, and shy, is the exact opposite of the idea many people have of him. But the real Adriano is the one I am describing, not the one of the collective imagination. Those who know him well know this is perfectly true. And I am deeply proud to be his friend today.

Tennis as a Personal Confrontation

Tennis is basically a personal confrontation. The rules are designed to determine who is the strongest, with no time limit and no possibility of a draw. Despite being a sport without physical contact, tennis is filled with tremendous emotional brutality. The rules of the gladiators in the Colosseum were much the same: one of the two contenders had to leave the arena "feet first". And it didn't matter how long it took.

In sports vocabulary we talk about "winning" or "losing," but in tennis, as far as my experience goes, we should talk about "surviving" or "dying". I know that Al Pacino in the role of a coach also evokes this in his famous speech to his football team. And I had sensed this ever since I was a boy, long before the movie *Any Given Sunday*.

The great Austrian scientist and father of psychoanalysis Sigmund Freud spoke of two lives, the rational life and the unconscious life, and it was to the latter that Freud associated tennis. Sexuality and aggressivity are the two motors of the unconscious that come from the internal impulse for the preservation of the species: sexuality for reproduction, and aggressivity for the defense of the offspring.

The latter is a key element, in my experience, to winning tennis matches. "Play aggressive!" is one of the most frequently heard pieces of advice from coaches all over the world. The tennis player has a great need for such aggressiveness. This is the inner drive he draws upon to find solutions, and where the energy to win the hardest fought matches is generated. The following story is emblematic of this view. I experienced this firsthand and felt the aggressivity that the events of the match triggered in me.

Gilbert Schaller, an Austrian, was truly a tough player. He was an outstanding athlete, with the physique of another era, with a very solid two-handed backhand and very good change of directions toward the down the line shot. He was my opponent in 1992 in Naples, Florida, in an ATP tournament.

The tournament was of average importance, but there were many participants because of its beautiful location. It was organized in a lovely but somewhat isolated luxury resort. The players, not having much else to do especially in the evening, became spectators too. 'The Bar' there, which in the U.S. is not a cafe for "cornetto and cappuccino" as in my Italian homeland, opened around ten at night more for beer and chatting up. My match against Schaller began at 8:00 p.m., and all the players who had already played would have tacitly planned to meet up at The Bar afterwards.

The Center Court was filled with American fans of a

certain age and already a little tipsy. I was in good shape. My forehand could destroy the "tennis wall" that my opponent was building in front of me. Indeed even though on clay, at Roland Garros, he had beaten even Pete Sampras. I had convinced myself that I could win. I was intent on playing each point very patiently before unleashing my famous winning forehand. The games were progressing very slowly. After more than an hour of play we were at 5-all.

On the 6-5 game point for me I shot a winner forehand, which landed near the line. It was called out. I approached the net to check the mark left by the ball, as is often the case in clay court matches, and the umpire confirmed the call. Out of nowhere, for no real reason other than his prejudice against Italians, Schaller shouted out in English, "You're not in Italy where you can rip off points". A public insult to me and my entire country. There was a loud buzz from the audience.

At that point, my adrenaline shot up and, in my mind, I turned a tense game into war. Seized with anger, I responded by attacking him personally: "Are you nervous because you're the ugliest guy on the circuit? You look like a Picasso painting," and, not content, I overstepped every possible limit of decency and added, "But did you become like that when you won the Chernobyl tournament?"

A few years earlier the tremendous nuclear explosion in Ukraine had threatened all of Europe. Austria was among the most exposed of the Western countries. It was a totally inappropriate, shocking joke, and I knew I was hurting him with my reference to it. Big laugh from the spectators, including all my colleagues who had sided with me from the beginning, partly because Schaller was not exactly the most popular person in the locker room.

The tension was suffocating. Again, some more very close points with exchanges of more than thirty shots. At the end of each point, a provocative gesture or shout from one to the other. I won the first set and at the change of ends, the physical confrontation was getting closer and closer. I also noticed that from the front row a woman spectator was constantly shouting things at me in German that sounded offensive, and I realized that she was Schaller's girlfriend.

Brian Earley, the tournament supervisor, was one of the most knowledgeable and experienced tennis professionals in the world. He sensed what was building up right away, and at the end of the first set called us under the umpire's chair. "If you don't stop, I'm going to throw both of you off the court. Now shake hands and apologize to each other if you want to continue the match". He was right. Schaller apologized for calling all the Italians thieves, and I apologized to him and said it wasn't true that he was the ugliest guy on the circuit. Brian got back next to the court and never moved again.

Gilbert Schaller by then was willing to do anything to win that match, and so was I. I lost the second 7-5 and it was already almost 11 p.m. Two sets of the match had taken three hours. Despite the hour, no one budged from their seat. Every point seemed to drag in its wake anger, competitive passion, and competitive hatred for the opponent. These were all the elements that attracted an audience, just like blood at the Colosseum.

Both of us just barely kept our behavior within acceptable

limits, but the tension was written all over our faces. It came down to the tie-break of the third set. By now it seemed more like a movie. Match point for me... not taken advantage of... then one for him which I saved with a winning serve... This went on until 11-10 for me in the tie-break of the third... and then he finally sent a forehand that was too long... I had never been so happy to have won a match in all my life.

I was screaming and jumping up and down and, as was the custom in the '70s, despite battling for four and a quarter hours, I jumped over the net to go to shake Schaller's hand. But once on the other side, intoxicated by my victory, I was swept away by the all-American custom of cranking up some music after a tennis match. Bad luck would have it that the notes of "Lambada", that was so wildly popular in '92, came booming over the Center Court.

And so it was that just an instant, only a split second before I was going to sportingly shake hands with my opponent, I suddenly got the urge to start dancing the lambada around him instead, to mock him for his defeat. This was accompanied by the audience's wild clapping. Schaller picked up his bag and did not speak to me for the next twenty years.

It only took me a few minutes to shower and I was ready to celebrate my victory at The Bar, even though I had the semifinal match the next day. As I entered, I was met by a standing ovation from my colleagues, thrilled by the unexpected evening entertainment they had been offered. Even today those present at Naples '92 remember and laugh about that memorable fight against Gilbert Schaller.

I would like to say that I do not think that I was a good

example at all for the young people who might read this story. And I sincerely apologize to Gilbert and his fiancée for my name-calling thirty-one years ago, even though he started it. I know I could have been just as aggressive without slipping into overly provocative behavior.

Yet it is also clear from this story that tennis is an extreme sport. To be able to survive on the court you have to be willing to die, emotionally speaking. High levels of aggressiveness and the will to engage in extreme struggle become as necessary as if you were in the jungle and armed only with a racket.

The Turbulent '90s of Tennis

For me the early '90s were characterized by Martin Simek, my coach during those years. He was Dutch by his passport, but a Czech from Prague, in then Czechoslovakia. I feel enormously indebted to Martin. He made me aware of how my experience as a professional tennis player had been of such great benefit to my inner personal growth, and that this was far more important than winning or losing. A few years later, once I became a coach myself, I would make this fundamental coaching principle my own. I am deeply convinced that my success and achievements in coaching are primarily rooted in this very principle.

In the early '90s I therefore began reading a lot more non-sports newspapers. I was following the political events of my country and of all the countries where my work took me at the time. I was becoming more selective, or at least trying to be, in relationships in my life.

The years 1991 and 1992 were good ones for me as a pro player, both in terms of my state of mind and my results.

In 1992 I won a match at Roland Garros against the Argentine-Belgian, Eduardo Masso, a tough left-hander who on clay would do anything to win. He was married to the daughter of Eddy Merckx, the strongest cyclist in history. It was often joked that Masso must have somehow taken after his father-in-law when it came to stamina on the court.

As for me, I had matured. I was no longer embroiled in relationships with selfish and insecure women (as I often had been). And during those years I had been able to absorb the best from my great coach, Martin Simek. Above and beyond being a coach, he was an artist, a great artist, and he had a decisive impact on my personal growth, my outlook on life and, consequently, my performance on the court.

At Roland Garros that winning year, every point was a marathon, one set each, until the fifth when, after five hours of play, I won. To describe the personal joy of winning a match at Roland Garros is not easy. One feels intimately satisfied and proud. You have the sweet certainty of having given more than everything on the court, of having delved into your body and mind to their farthest recesses to find the energy needed. You are aware that your opponent on the other side of the net had been doing the same.

Eduardo Masso and I were, and are, very close friends. Also because, not to be underestimated, we had won an important doubles match together at the Bordeaux tournament against Canè and Colombo. At the time they were the titular doubles pair in Davis and one of the strongest pairs in the world.

We hugged and talked about the match. After my massage, I went back to my room at the Hotel Concorde Lafayette, a towering hotel in Paris located at the end of the wonderful Champs-Élysées. Rarely had I felt so satisfied in my life and so aware of my strength. I tossed my briefcase and duffel bag into a corner of my tiny room, threw myself on the bed for a well-deserved rest before dinner, turned on the TV overhead and went straight to the RAI channel, which in Paris, miraculously, had a signal... It was May 23, 1992.

I saw "Special Edition" – a highway and lots of smoke. The broken voice of the RAI journalist talking about Judge Falcone and his wife Francesca Morvillo, and the young men of the security team having been "blown up" on the highway at Capaci, Palermo.

I have always taken my being Italian very seriously and very deeply. When I was the starter of the Italian Davis Cup team and Mameli's national anthem started to play, I could not hold back the tears of pride, as always, for the honor of representing Italy. I would do anything in my power to bring my country prestige in sports. When the verse of "*siam pronti alla morte*" came, I felt that if it were ever necessary, yes, I would give my life for Italy. My love, and the gratitude of having been born in Rome, its capital, are immense.

But at that moment, in Paris, the brutal shift from the pride of having won a match at Roland Garros and honored Italy, to the devastating disappointment of my country's failure as the 'sovereign democratic state' I thought I represented, was a shock. I felt a violent jolt in my chest, my heart leapt just as it had during the match point a few hours before at Porte d'Auteuil, at Roland Garros. I wept in despair, this time in pain, thinking of Italy, the country that was betraying us.

I had the feeling, like a premonition, that the State had somehow been involved, and that the mafia had been more an accomplice than an enemy. I thought of Dalla Chiesa. And Pio La Torre, whose young daughter had been a ball girl at the Palermo Tournament. I really loved that tournament. With spineless mockery my fellow foreign tennis players had called it the "Mafia Open". It was as if I already knew how right Magistrate Caponnetto was, when in one of his famous interviews after the assassination of Judge Borsellino a few months later, in July, he had said, "It's all over".

Even today, those responsible for that period of massacres is still not entirely clear. What does this have to do with tennis? It has so much to do with it, because in tennis the sense of belonging to a homeland is very strong. This is true whether at the Davis Cup or in individual tournaments where your country's flag is always displayed on the scoreboards next to your name.

Yet as Giovanni Falcone himself once said, "One must not confuse respect for the institutions with respect for those who represent them at a particular moment". I began to think about moving abroad. After waiting perhaps too long, because of my deep attachment to my country, I took up residence in the United States of America.

That day of May 23 was also a turning point in my life. My negative state of mind contributed in no small way to my losing the next match I played at Roland Garros. It was against a Croatian, Goran Prpic, who was strong, but against whom I had no doubts I could win.

Two Extraordinary Events in My City

There is a tennis tournament in Rome held in May at the Foro Italico facility adjacent to the Olympic Stadium. This is a wonderful tradition that grew in leaps and bounds during the '70s thanks to Adriano Panatta, who was born in Rome. In 1976 Panatta was the last Italian to win the tournament. To me, even since I was a youngster, this tournament was by far the most important tennis event ever. And this is how thousands of Roman tennis players of all levels and all ages felt too. People talked about the tournament all year around, and not just about the matches. This is still the case even today.

In the booming '70s of tennis, everyone in Rome played. New tennis clubs were cropping up every day. You lived and breathed tennis everywhere. The International Championships of Italy were as fascinating on the court, on the sports side, as off the court, on the social side. Many romances between Rome's sweethearts began during the event. It was impressive just to simply say, "I've got tickets, this year I'm going to the Foro Italico to watch tennis," Let alone for me, a Roman, to play in the tournament and even win matches in front of my whole city. For a few years I was the eighth King of Rome, and there was no shortage of fans' banners waving on the Center Court to remind everyone of it.

Of course this was not comparable to Adriano Panatta's popularity during his era, though I was supposed to be heir to his legacy. In any case, failing that, I apparently did leave some unforgettable moments with the public, judging from the welcome I am still honored with in practically all the circles of the Capital. It makes me realize that I must have left some strong memories with people during that span of six or seven years.

In 1992 two extraordinary tennis events took place in my city. The first, of course, was the Forum Tournament. I had participated in April in a series of very important ATP tournaments in the U.S. I felt at home in that country and many years later, in middle age, I went to live there. The last of the ATP tournaments was held in Atlanta, Georgia. I took my flight back to Rome. My grandfather Ernesto, a butcher by profession and former Fortitudo soccer player, had been a charismatic figure in Rome's Flaminio neighborhood since the 1920s. His team Fortitudo, which merged with Virtus in 1927, had given birth to the Roma Soccer Team...

Just minutes before I landed at Rome's Fiumicino airport, Grandpa Ernesto passed away in the Villa San Pietro Hospital. I had missed being able to say goodbye to him only by a few hours. I wept in despair, alone, in the parking lot of the hospital. He had been my very first fan. Although he knew little, if anything, about tennis, no customer at the butcher shop had ever left without hearing all about my exploits.

It was a Saturday, and the following Monday would be the beginning of my most emotionally intense tournament ever. That is, the Rome Tournament. But Monday was also the day of Grandpa Ernesto's funeral in the nearby church of Santa Croce on Via Guido Reni. I asked and was allowed to play the first round on Tuesday. This was against a very strong player from Spain who ranked among the world's top sixty, German Lopez.

I played an exceptional game and won 6-3, 6-4. My grandmother Enrica, grieving the loss of her husband, but as usual with a smile, and her positive attitude about life, was there, as well as Uncle Vittorio, a former Lazio soccer player of the '60s, who had returned from Canada. I hugged all my family and prepared for the second round. This would get me into the round of 16, and I was up against a very tough Dutchman, Mark Koevermans.

Incredibly, the match was scheduled on Court 4. I never understood why, it made no sense, even from the point of view of keeping public order. The stands were packed, not only on my court, but on the other side of it too, that is, where the spectators were supposed to be watching Court 5. Instead, they had gone to cheer me on from over there. The players on 5 found it enormously difficult to play because of this. They had to compete with an audience "out of sync", since the spectators were watching another game. I was sure

I had also seen a couple of kids who had even climbed up one of the pine trees to watch my game.

I thought of my grandfather and my pre-emptive guilt, which foolishly made me feel that if I lost, I would not honor his memory worthily. I was playing with ups and downs, and Koevermans, a great athlete and very mean on the court, took a 4-1 lead in the third set. As I sat during the change of courts, I had given up all hope of a comeback. I wondered why the level of my playing for one reason or another could never really take off.

A chant started up from the grandstand... at first only by one spectator, but then the chorus grew and grew, as the thousands of fans made it turn into a deafening roar... It was the encouraging *Alee...o-o, Alee...o-o* that Claudio Baglioni exalted in his songs... In fact, I recalled that I had only just recently met the great singer himself. He and I shared the same athletic trainer, the great Aureliano Musulin.

Something happened inside of me. My heart started beating faster, and suddenly my lucidity at the game became extremely focused. I got back to 4 even. The people were beside themselves and me too, with them. My audience and I were playing that match together. Mark Koevermans from Rotterdam was scared. At 5-4 for me I was sure to break again. I got to match point and my opponent again made the right choice. He attacked me on the backhand. Yet I, in my full state of grace, came at full speed running to the left and threw a longline passing shot worthy of Ken Rosewall.

I won the game by sliding under the crowd of people who had dangerously flocked into the corner where I had ended up hitting that passing shot. I will never forget it for the rest of my life. I looked at the sky then, and smiled. I was thinking of how happy Grandpa Ernesto would have been. Many people were in tears, and even I was caught in a strange fit of laughing and crying all at once. Koevermans was enraged and was talking to himself, cursing in Dutch...

I then lost in the round of 16. Nevertheless, the mission was accomplished – in fact, doubly so. I had paid homage to my grandfather very worthily, and I had played a very special tournament in my city to be remembered forever. A few months later, the popularity I enjoyed from that match in my hometown came to my rescue, though of course I could never have imagined in what way it would.

The second tennis event was in November, again in Rome, but in a completely different setting. It was played in the EUR sports palace, a structure on the opposite side of town that had been built for the 1960 Rome Olympics. The event was promoted in the newspapers as an "Exhibition", a term I had never liked. It was called the "Big 4". The World Top 4 players would compete in a mini tournament of semifinals and finals. This was in preparation for the ATP Masters, the year-end event of the Top 8 in the ATP rankings, which, in importance, was comparable to a Grand Slam tournament.

In 1992 the Top 4 players were Becker, Edberg, Sampras and Ivanisevic. I was asked if I wanted to train with them during the week. I was in Rome and a level sparring partner, being in the World Top 8. The champions, who were all my friends, except Sampras, whom I didn't know as well, would have liked that. Needless to say, I eagerly accepted and spent the week with the world tennis elite as training partners. It was so much fun to go to my clubhouse in the morning and tell my friends at the bar that I would train with Edberg and Becker that afternoon, and the next day with Sampras, and so on...

The evening of official matches came. At 8 p.m. Ivanisevic vs. Edberg would begin, followed by Becker vs. Sampras. About 7:00 that evening, however, Sergio Palmieri, the tournament director, called me on his mobile with what would be shocking news to all of us in those early 1990s. "Claudio," he said to me in a very low voice, "what are you doing tonight? I thought he was going to offer me free tickets to watch the matches. "I'm coming to the Pala EUR, would you have tickets for me?" "Becker has a fever and has withdrawn, I desperately need your help. The only chance to calm down the paying public is for you to play against Sampras – would you be okay with five million lire (about 5,000 dollars) ?"

I was speechless and felt like I had been punched in the stomach, but out of joy. "That's fine, I'm coming". My father brought me my rackets and competition clothes. I found myself before twenty thousand people who had just been told that after spending eighty thousand liras (about 80 dollars) for their ticket, they would not see the great Boris play. I entered the court and Palmieri put the microphone in my hand to explain directly to the Romans that it would be me playing instead of Becker. He probably would not have had the courage.

The five seconds of silence it took me to find the words seemed like a scene from a play. "Ahó!" – and with that all-

Roman greeting I was already getting all the twenty thousand people there on my side... "I was already very happy tonight to have free tickets, and then twenty minutes ago they told me I have to play..." Everyone laughed and Sampras looked very bewildered. "I will do my best to look like Becker, in fact I was even looking for a blond wig ..." and the house came down with another great laugh. I saw the immense relief on Palmieri's face.

I had been able to save the evening mainly because six months earlier on the court at the Foro Italico I had earned the esteem forever of my fellow citizens. I told Sampras, whose nickname was "Pistol Pete", that the original "Pistol" was me, since they were the first six letters of my last name, and I was four years older than him. He laughed heartily too, and we played a good match. He won 6-3, 6-2, but with many good points by me. My innate irony, as a true Roman, and the all-Roman ability to never take anything too seriously, had saved the tournament.

In Milan as winner of the Avvenire Doubles Tournament with my friend Giuseppe Tesorone. The Tournament is still today one of the world's most important for Under-16 players.

Handshake with 1988 World No. 1 champion Mats Wilander, after defeating him at the Monte Carlo Tournament of that year. This was the most prestigious victory of my career.

Snapshots from my life as tennis player and coach.
Clockwise from top: with friend Boris Becker at the Doha Tournament in 1991; with Roger Federer, my first President on the ATP Player Council (today called ATP Player Advisory Council) when I was Coach Representative; with champion Daniela Hantuchova; Andre Agassi in 1992 in Tampa, Florida; with Novak Djokovic, my second President as Coach Representative on the ATP Player Council.

The great honor of being awarded 1985 Junior World Champion by Rod Laver.

In 2002 a taste of victory with a trophy received at the Palalido of Milan as Davide Sanguinetti's coach. Sanguinetti had just defeated Roger Federer.

The Japanese winners of the 2006 Japan Doubles Open, Satoshi Iwabuchi and Takao Suzuki (left). I coached Takao for fourteen years and with him we opened the doors to international tennis for Japan during the 2000s.

My backhand. This was sometimes referred to as my weak point when compared to my forehand. But this was not true. It was a strong backhand, even though my playing hinged on my forehand.

© 2023 Ray Giubilo

My forehand. My trademark. This is what I became known for in all the international professional tennis world.

© 2023 Ray Giubilo

With Paolo Bertolucci and Roberto Lombardi, two technical professionals who accompanied me with dedication and professionalism as I climbed from Junior to Professional tennis player.

Foto Angelo Tonelli

With the trophy of the 1990 Italian Championship.
I will always feel the pride of having been an Italian Championship winner.

At Wimbledon as coach of the 2008 No. 1 in Italy, Simone Bolelli.
I coached an Italian tennis player right up to the nation's top twice,
the other player being Davide Sanguinetti (2002).

I had the privilege dozens of times
of being on the court with Roger Federer.

As Robin Söderling's coach in the 2011 Brisbane Tournament.
Three consecutive ATP Tournament victories in 2011 – Brisbane, Rotterdam and Marseille – and "Best Ranking" for Robin Söderling as World No. 4.

The Triumph of Milan 2002

Milan 2002, Palalido, Piazzale Lotto.

Davide Sanguinetti won the tournament in the final against Roger Federer. It had been a triumphant week for Sanguinetti that Roger himself, yes that very Roger, often liked to relive with me when he stopped by at tournaments for a friendly chat.

That week Davide had experienced "flow", that inexplicable state of grace. The greatest players may experience this quite frequently throughout the year. In 2002 Davide had begun laying the foundations to becoming a top player himself, or at least certainly among the World Top 10.

Yet the tournament hadn't gotten off to a good start for Davide... He went into the first round without having found his inner equilibrium. He was playing against a German, a certain Christian Vink, whom I had beaten seven years before in a minor tournament in the Philippines. Vink was famous for having beaten "The Las Vegas Kid", Andre Agassi, in the U.S. in a Challenger Tournament. This had been during Agassi's most serious slump.

We were now down a break in the third. I looked at Davide's wife Tatiana sitting next to me, and she was pensive but calm. She had the serene expression that only a woman expecting a child could have. Tatiana was a true Roman like me, and it only took half a glance to understand each other. She was saying something like "No problem, if he loses let's go home and enjoy the family". As unexpected as it was fortuitous, Davide, like the great fighter he is, even when it comes to confronting his own self, managed a couple of his legendary two-handed backhand winners. He somehow won the match. He then won his second-round match against Juan Carlos Ferrero, World No. 3 at the time.

I will never forget the practice session the next day at Milan Harbour, the most exclusive club in Milan. Davide played from memory, didn't say a word, didn't complain, and his every shot turned into a winner. He won a practice set 6-0 and, unlike me usually, I didn't say a thing for the whole set either. Afterwards, I went over to him. A little hesitantly, I offer some comments on a few aspects, such as his serve, that had improved thanks to a small step in the preparation phase. It was an idea that had already worked brilliantly with other players I had coached. He stopped me, gently but very firmly, "Claudio", he put a hand on my arm, "don't say a thing to me, I feel everything was perfect".

He was right, David was a "feeling" player, one who feels how things are. He gives his best when everything is right around him. A coach must understand when to be close to the player but leave room for this "feeling". Davide won 6-2, 6-3 against Ferrero, playing truly stellar tennis.

Then Davide beat Younes El Aynaoui who was a very strong Moroccan player, at the time among the World Top 20. El Aynaoui had the support of his compatriots' tremendous cheering in the stadium. They were Moroccans living in Milan who had come out in impressive numbers to the Palalido on Piazzale Lotto.

Davide's tennis was like a symphony in which everything was perfectly orchestrated. Loose serve, but great acceleration. The forehand, his weak point, worked with the "fisherman's technique". That was an analogy I had made up to explain to him how the shoulder should be stretched forward to give penetration and control to the shot, like a fisherman with his rod when he wants to cast bait far out at sea. As I watched the match, I thought his backhand was the best of all time among Italian players who execute this shot with two hands. I still think so today too, in the hope that Seppi and Sinner won't mind.

Even on the bench we were in perfect harmony. I was not only Davide's coach, but a friend and a brother to him. This bond went back to the time we played against each other, and he was just a youngster. I beat him, but we found out we were both born on the same day, August 25, although with five years difference. And beside me, there was his wife Tatiana, so sweet but also very direct and with a profound look in her eyes. Their infant Alice, in her tummy, was born a few weeks later.

Fighting like a lion, at crucial moments Davide achieved

even higher levels in his play. The next day he won against the French player Nicolas Escudé who was a Top 20 and semifinalist at the Australian Open of that year. I got a chill just thinking of the final... Davide still had a match to win before savoring the triumph, and on the way the obstacle would be the defending champion, a young Swiss player in his twenties with a brilliant and lethal game. His name was Roger Federer...

RAI was there to cover the tournament and Italia 1 too. The Palalido was jam-packed, and, to my delight, there were a lot of kids. I chatted for a while with Mediaset journalist Lucia Blini. She was beautiful, professional and elegant in every way and very popular as copresenter with the famous Sandro Piccinini of Mediaset's iconic soccer program of those years, "Controcampo".

As I sat in the coach's box, I noticed that Corrado Barazzutti was trying to slip in to sit next to me to be strategically positioned for the camera. "Barazza", also nicknamed "Barracuda" or "little soldier" (the latter, in my opinion, was the more apt nickname) had been a great champion player. He was at the Milan tournament, though, as Davis Cup captain.

I have crossed paths with thousands of people in my life, and some have disappointed me, but I am sorry to say that Corrado Barazzutti disappointed me more than any other. I say this, though still recognize his tremendous merit as a player. Indeed, he was decisive in the great victories of "the Team" in the '70s. I'll skip the details, but there was already enough tension in our box so I politely asked him to leave.

Davide, once again, surpassed himself at decisive moments and won in three sets. Roger paid for his ups and downs and was also amazed at Davide's extraordinary forehand and serve. These were the two strokes we had been working on for two years, based on expertise and determination. It was a triumph. As Davide gave his speech, I ducked under the stands so that he would not see me weeping for joy. It didn't seem real to me. An Italian player that I had coached winning the historic Milan tournament.

It was a tournament that had been won in the past by the likes of McEnroe, Edberg, and Becker, and the previous year by Roger Federer. Yet at the time we did not know that Roger, who had just lost to Davide, would greatly surpass all three of those other players... I was thirty-four, still young enough to compete, but that victory confirmed to me that I had made the right decision to withdraw from playing. Though it was a few years earlier than expected, I had been able to begin paving the way to an exceptional coaching career.

I found myself in the darkened locker room after the match with Davide and Roger. As Davide left for the ritual press conference, I remained there with an extremely disappointed Roger". Coach, did he play well, or did I play badly?" he asked. "David played the best game of his life. He has been in a state of grace ever since the second round, but today against you he outdid himself, especially in the decisive moments" I explained.

"You had a few ups and downs, and I'm not surprised, I knew Peter Carter well (the South African coach with whom Roger grew up as a Junior, and who died in a car accident) ...

and he prepared you so well for your career ... so you don't have to worry about anything. You have great strokes and if you work well with your coach, in my opinion, you're going to the World Top 5 for sure..."

I could read by his expression that he greatly appreciated my encouragement. He was already dreaming of seeing his name among the Top 5... After his defeat that day though, he would barely be ranked among the Top 20. Roger did not even remotely suspect that he was destined to win twenty Slam tournaments and that over the next twenty years, as a player, he would write the most important pages in the history of our sport. I was not wrong when I predicted to Roger, "I'm sure you'll make it to the World Top 5, don't worry," though if I point this out today no one takes it seriously...

Two Standing Ovations in One Day in New York

Salerno 1990.

The Italian Absolute Championships began in September and for the first round I was to play against Davide Sanguinetti, an 18-year-old from La Spezia. "Watch out, he trains in the States and plays well," a fellow player friend warned me. But I was feeling relaxed and in good form. It was a period when I was single, a respite between girlfriends, and during those times it so happens I almost always achieved my best results.

Not knowing my opponent, I started that first round playing on his backhand – how could I have known that despite his young age, I was up against the best two-handed backhand in the history of Italian tennis. On his second, or at most third backhand, Davide got me with his backhand winner down the line. He did this so simply, as if he were just playing for practice. I had challenged and defeated two-handed backhanders such as Wilander or Bruguera, Kent Carlsson or Aaron Krickstein, but nothing could compare with the fluidity and precision of the backhand of this youth from La Spezia.

Perhaps only the backhand of Miloslav Mecir, known as "Big Cat," or Andre Agassi's had had a more devastating effect on my game.

In just a moment I was down 4-1. He let out a shout, justified, but in a defiant tone, and this irritated me to no end. I called him over to the net and said menacingly, "A ragazzi', you know you have to show respect for your elders don't you?" He hadn't done anything really disrespectful, but partly out of pride, partly because I knew I was in a position to intimidate him, I launched into that somewhat harsh "warning". But it worked. His courage wavered, and I won 6-4, 6-1, 6-1. This was also because I had finally realized that I had to stay away from that backhand of his.

I liked him very much. He told me he was training in Florida and that he wanted to go to college in the States. In fact, he later became a legend on the UCLA team, the famous Bruins with which Arthur Ashe and Jimmy Connors had also played. The match Davide and I played that day was at the Le Querce club in Salerno, my stomping grounds. The Center Court was carved out of a natural basin overlooking the sea and the view was breathtaking. Little did I know that this was only the beginning of a bond between Davide and I that would lead to truly unforgettable moments for both of us. In 1998 he asked me to be his coach, and I coached him until 2008.

The tournament that truly makes my heart race when I think of it is the 2005 U.S. Open. A curious coincidence was that August 25 marked both Davide's and my birthdays. For many years, on the eve of the tournament held between

August and September, Davide and I would always celebrate our birthdays together at the same restaurant.

That restaurant also plays a role in another incredible coaching story of my life. In 1996 Takao Suzuki took me for the first time to the very famous Japanese restaurant, "Nippon". It still exists today, on 52nd Street between Lexington and Third Avenue in Manhattan. For twenty-five years I have always celebrated my birthdays at "Nippon" and have become like one of the family.

Back to the U.S. Open. Davide started in the first round against Wayne Arthurs, an Australian left-hander who was famous for his extremely powerful and accurate serves that were virtually impossible to return. What Arthurs, very nice fellow by the way, did not expect was that Davide was one of the players with the best "sixth sense" in service returns. Nothing predictable or coachable, just pure 24-carat instinct. Davide would follow his intuition and anticipate. I saw him do this against Edberg and Sampras as well and in fact throughout his entire career.

That day it wasn't much of a struggle to bring the match home. He could now prepare to face one of the best players of all time, the recent World No. 1, Carlos Moyá.

Just as in Milan three years before, when Davide had won the final against Roger Federer, I knew there were certain weeks when silence or very few short but strong phrases, were the best support for him. Giving space to his instincts, not making him think, but rather making him "feel" the game. I had been right this time too. The match was soon in Davide's favor. He was stealing time from Moyá, not letting him control the center of the court with his legendary forehand, and attacking him hard on the second service ball: 2 sets to 1 for Davide, and a two break lead.

It only took a nanosecond for Davide's wife Tatiana (who as mentioned was a Roman like me) and I to share what we were both thinking. In a glance we told each other that Davide was in his "magic flow" again, and anything could happen in this tournament. Even three-year-old Alice, their daughter, was smiling. Suddenly I saw Davide give up taking a ball that was two steps away from him. Then another one... He lost one of his two breaks, and in less than a minute we had a new match. Moyá yelled the very dangerous "Vamos!" like a Spanish war cry. Davide walked to the changeover chair. I looked over at him and yelled, "If you're sick, call for a physio!"

He shook his head "No", then exclaimed, "Look!" Davide lifted one foot and I saw that the sole of his shoe was almost completely eaten away. He had been playing on a burning court in the 37-degree-Celsius in-the-shade heat and was running virtually just on his sock. "You have an extra pair of shoes, don't you?!" Every self-respecting professional carries a pair of spare shoes in his bag. Davide was often a little lax, shall we say, on the organizational side. No, he didn't have any.

For those of you unfamiliar with the USTA Billie Jean King National Tennis Center in Flushing Meadows, the locker rooms are in the "belly" of the main Arthur Ashe Stadium. This was at least a fifteen-minute walk from the outside courts. So, from Court 7, where we were, Davide had the choice of either continuing the match on one shoe and his sock, or losing the match by withdrawal.

Thank goodness Davide and I had a lot in common and that we were like twins. As mentioned, we were even born on the same day (although five years apart). We had the same sponsor and, what was more, we had the same shoe size. I immediately thought of throwing Davide my left shoe from the stands, but I couldn't remember whether I had come to the match in tennis shoes or running shoes. I was afraid to even look – but they were tennis shoes! Time seemed to stop for a few seconds for what happened next. "Davideeee! Here's a shoe!"

I was standing next to Tatiana at the top of the grandstand and she covered her eyes, afraid to even look. My throw, in front of everyone, including the TV viewers, was perfect. The shoe flew a good twenty meters down and landed in Davide's hands, as he stood laughing. Moyá followed the scene with his mouth agape just like everyone else. It was all just pure formality after that, as Davide finished the fourth set, and then won the match 6 games to 3. This got us into the third round, against Paradorn Shrichapan. He was World No. 7 and the strongest Asian player of all time.

Two days later we were given the Armstrong Court at the U.S. Open for the match against Paradorn. The former Center Court at Flushing Meadows stirred intense memories of the most exciting moments of tennis. This was the court of John McEnroe's triumphs. He was there that day at our match as commentator. Davide, a.k.a. "Dado," was warming up precisely where almost twenty years before, when I was nineteen, I had challenged Jimmy Connors. I had forced him into a more than three-hour struggle. As I travelled back in time, I could see the 14,000 supporters rooting for "Jimbo" Connors, and I remembered how this had not managed to intimidate me.

The match began a few hours later and one corner of the Armstrong stands had turned all red... Paradorn Shrichapan was from Thailand, and he had become a national hero and was a personal friend of the King. Red was the color of battle in his country. The thousands of Thais, who had travelled all the way to New York to hail their hero, were indeed ready for battle.

Davide, at the age of thirty-three, could not have found himself in worse circumstances. Down two sets, both lost in tie-break after two and a half hours. During those twenty shots per point, he had spent enormous energy against an opponent known to be an incomparable athlete. It was even said that Paradorn, only a year before, had also been the Asian vice-champion in Thai Boxing.

Indeed, Schrichapan closed the set point of the second set with a volley played in a full split. He had that kind of flexibility seen only in martial arts champions. He then thought it best to do ten lightning quick push-ups. This was a little to mock the "old man" Sanguinetti whose sideburns were growing a bit grey, we might add. Anyway, he had never done that...!

Davide looked at me with his eyes wide open, as if to say, "I swear if it kills me, I'm going to win this match!" Dado is the gentlest, kindest and most tender person in the world, but on the court, if provoked, he becomes a killer, a pit bull that won't let go even if shot. With a sigh I said to Tatiana, "I think he's right. He's going to win this match".

And Dado won the hard fought third set, raging, as he

made a volley that spun back into his court. In all the eight years I had coached him, he must have tried that at least thirty times without, to my despair, ever succeeding. But that day, he even did that too. It was a signal. Well over four hours passed and we went into the fifth set. No one budged and the thousands of Thais were by now starting to get a little nervous. They had thought after the two sets that it was in the bag. They started to shout their soccer chants, in Thai, even louder. I noticed that at the Center Court, where the great Kim Clijsters was playing, hundreds of spectators had now gone up to the top seats to see Davide's match instead, and were leaning dangerously over the railing.

The fifth set continued at a palpitating pace. After the tournament, John McEnroe claimed that in his opinion that match had been the best of the entire 2005 U.S. Open. This was a tremendous compliment for Davide. At the tie-break of the fifth set I had noticed some aspiring Italian journalists. Though usually rather defeatist and sarcastic in those days when it came to their home tennis players, they seemed to have shed all their defenses and frustrations and were cheering at the top of their lungs for Davide.

After five hours and fifteen minutes, Davide punched his ticket to the round of 16 in New York, just like Adriano Panatta had done. He got a well-deserved standing ovation from the whole stadium as he came over to hug me. Certainly, that had to be one of the most beautiful victories in the history of Italian tennis at the U.S. Championships, a Grand Slam tournament. To me, along with Wimbledon, it was the most important tournament in the world.

It was late by the time Davide had had his massage and the press conference was over. It was going to be a feat finding a restaurant open in Manhattan at that hour. In the end, we were recommended to a jam-packed renowned Italian restaurant. They were broadcasting the U.S. Open on the many screens around the tables. Davide, his wife Tatiana, their little girl Alice, and I went inside. Davide and I were in our tennis clothes, our eyes bloodshot with exhaustion.

Everyone turned to look at us. The customers, one by one, began standing up, applauding. Davide turned around, genuinely convinced that a famous actor or someone like that was coming in behind us. Instead, that second standing ovation of the day was actually for us! We burst into tears, in a mixture of relief after the tremendous nervous tension we had accumulated during that endless day, and the joy at such recognition for our work. That was the kind of tribute that remains in your heart for life, and that no trophy, official award, prestigious title or roll of honor can ever equal.

For the records, Davide lost the round of 16 to David Nalbandian in four sets, though not without winning the first set, again, in a tie-break.

Let Me Tell You about Roger Federer

"*Ciao Grande*!"

Yes, that's Roger Federer. Not only has he always stopped to chat, but when he sees me, he always calls me "Grande!" Yes, Federer calls *me* "Great"...! I look back and focus on a handful of episodes that at the time had not seemed particularly extraordinary. Yet on that day in September 2022, during the Laver Cup, a poignant ceremony took place. It was the farewell to tennis of the man who among all others had been the most dominant figure in the sport. On that occasion, the memory of those episodes seemed to take on a completely different significance.

My memories of the great Federer seem as if looped together to span a period of at least twenty years. They leap here and there through time, but when it comes to Roger, this is not really important.

In 1999, at Charles De Gaulle Airport the organization of transfers for players and coaches to Roland Garros was not as effective as it is today. Technology was not yet up to handling all the problems of logistics. I spotted a sign with "Pestolezzi," as usual my last name was misspelled, just as it was mispronounced by the French, but at least this meant that I had a car and driver. I was to be taken to the Porte d'Auteuil where I was coaching Takao Suzuki and Davide Sanguinetti.

At Arrivals, there was this guy with a Wilson tennis bag, looking a little lost, so I asked, "Would you like a ride with me to Roland Garros?" "Yes thank you! If it's okay with you!" he said gratefully. He was polite and a little hesitant, unsure if this were against any rules. I turned to the driver, who nodded that it was okay. I reassured him "*Viens, il n'y a pas de problème*". "*Merci Monsieur, je m'appelle Roger*". And that was the first time I had ever spoken to him...

Flushing Meadows U.S. Open 2003. Any of the world's top players were available for workouts when it came to Davide Sanguinetti. Davide hit the ball cleanly and smoothly, ran on every ball, and was, and is, an extremely empathetic and kind person. Everyone felt it was a pleasure to train with Davide, and Roger Federer was no exception.

At the U.S. Open, the most coveted practice courts are P1 through P5. Located right beneath Arthur Ashe Stadium that had been built in 1997, they were just steps away from the locker rooms, gym and restaurant. These were the three key points where a tennis player spent his or her days during tournaments. The P stands for 'Practice', in keeping with the Americans' love it seems for abbreviating everything into an initial or an acronym.

At ten in the morning, very early by tennis standards, Davide had a workout with Federer, who was accompanied by Peter Lundgren, his coach at the time, and a great friend of mine. We two coaches, as was customary, began to open the new balls. Since the steel blade top that seals these tubes is very sharp, the coaches do this to avoid the risk of having the players cut their hands.

We were in awe before the majesty of what was the world's largest tennis stadium (yes, just like in Venditti's song "Roma Capoccia" that renders homage to the majesty of the Colosseum). The New York tennis stadium was dedicated to the great Arthur Ashe, who had passed away only a few years earlier. Like all coaches, I always have a dozen used balls in my bag. It was just a split second... the irresistible competitiveness of all tennis players (and former ones, which is the same thing), instinctively clicked in all of us. "What do you think? Can we hit a ball over to the stadium?" I had read everyone's mind.

Davide didn't have to give it a second thought. He took a used ball from my bag, calculated the distance to the very high wall of the stadium next to us, warmed up his wrist a little, and then hit the ball really hard upwards. The ball touched the wall about five meters below the rim. Then it was my turn, same result... Peter, the former World No. 25, didn't fare any better. Roger looked at us and laughed (Roger always laughed a lot) and I already knew how it was all going to end.

After two or three failed attempts by each of us, Roger grabbed a couple of the balls. The first, a test, fell a little short of the top of the wall. He took a deep breath, looked at the wall again as he always did before serving... stepped back, and fired a forehand upward with such extraordinary force that it was obvious it greatly surpassed any of our's. The ball sailed easily over the top of the wall, ending its parabolic path well inside the empty stands of the Arthur Ashe Stadium...

More than a quarter of an hour of training had already passed, but in fact we had already worked on a fundamental aspect of it, that is, the training of that personal sense of competition, challenge and confrontation which is the lifeblood of our sport. And I watched Roger as he used as leverage his sheer joy of being on a tennis court, out of pure love for this sport, to effortlessly find his way to victory. Whether it was winning the U.S. Open (which in fact that year he did) or the childish "Who can hit the ball over to the stadium", it was all the same to him.

I think Roger Federer was unique because he never lost the child in him, even while being extraordinarily professional and demanding in his work and training. It was that side of him that took such joy simply in "playing," in the most joyful sense of the word that enabled him to do whatever he desired with a ball and racket. It was what allowed him to sail over the mountain of expectations that the whole tennis world had of him... expectations of constant victory, of being perfect on any surface and in any tournament.

But I will talk more of Federer a little later on.

The Great Adventure of Life and Tennis in the Land of the Rising Sun

From a cultural point of view, it would appear that nothing could be further apart in terms of lifestyle, personal habits, or attitudes towards work and family, than someone "de Roma" and someone from Sapporo, a city in northern Japan and the capital of the island of Hokkaido. Yet, in my extraordinary globetrotter's life, I happened to meet a junior tennis player (i.e., under the age of eighteen), Takao Suzuki, at Roland Garros who would set milestones in my long career as a sportsman.

The greatest adventure of my life, in terms of personal growth, was about to begin, though I was still far from being aware of it. A kindly Japanese gentleman, accompanied by Dennis Van der Meer and his wife Pat, met me at the Concorde Lafayette hotel, near the Arc de Triomphe. There we were in Paris, a city whose beauty had always filled me with great positive energy. In 1996 I was going through a phase of great uncertainty. The previous year I had undergone herniated disc surgery. At the time this required nine months of convalescence.

The opinion of many, mainly ignorant and uninformed sources, was that at age twenty-nine it would be better to start thinking of giving up my career. In fact, after my back surgery, I had dropped from a solid ATP ranking in the Top 100 in the professional tennis rankings, to the position of a shaky 150 or worse. This meant I had gone from earning an income comparable to a professional such as a doctor or lawyer, to the limbo of semi-professionalism, where after expenses, there is barely enough to live a decent life on. As a player, I had never been very good at choosing who to trust for advice on the managerial level. Fortunately, however I was very good at choosing my coaches.

For a professional athlete, the ATP ranking is his occupational identity status. If you fell out of the Top 100, especially at the time, you knew that calling yourself a "professional" tennis player was a lie. You could still be in the Top 200 and get by on the minor circuit, playing "Challenger," or you could play in various team leagues in Europe. Unlike other sports, in tennis you can compete in the Italian league, and during the same year also in the German tennis league (Bundesliga), in the French league, or in any other country's league that has tennis clubs willing to pay a generous fee if you play a certain number of matches for their club. You become, in effect, a mercenary.

That was the dismal situation I found myself in. And for players at this level, tennis, whether in Italy or around the world, has been an organizational failure for decades. Only in recent years has there been an attempt to improve things, but there is still a long way to go.

I signed up for a series of tournaments in Holland. They were small tournaments, but that was all I could afford in order to move up the rankings. It was called a "satellite circuit" but I never quite understood why. The circuit was comprised of four consecutive tournaments and in the end players would be ranked according to who had the most "circuit points". ATP points would be distributed accordingly. It was mainly useful for aspiring players entering the world of tournaments with ATP points up for grabs. A twenty-nine-year-old with a long history in the Top 100 jarred the profile a bit.

"Claudio," the Japanese manager said to me, "I know you are not a coach, but Takao, who is only eighteen, is entered in the same tournaments in Holland. It would be so good for him if you could help him, play doubles with him, teach him how to play on clay, something he has never done in his life... and another thing... he speaks very little English". I was taken aback for a minute. My whole life seemed to pass before me, and for the first time I was seeing myself not as a pro player, but as a coach, and I liked that very much.

I asked for a night to think it over. That night I spent weeping over the realization that my tennis career was over, yet at the same time, I was swept up in volcanic enthusiasm. I saw the prospect of a new career suddenly opening up, one that would give me the chance to earn a living, and for which I definitely felt an inclination. The next morning, I accepted. I had taken my first step towards a new profession, though no one knew it yet.

We rented a car, a black Fiat Bravo, and I had some Eros Ramazzotti cassettes with me, which Takao loved. And so I found myself with this boy from Sapporo singing *"Più bella cosa"* at the top of his lungs and at the same time teaching him Italian. The affinity between the two of us, despite the stellar differences in culture and customs, was phenomenal.

It wasn't that I was particularly such a fan of Eros'. During those years I spent with that merry, fun loving and very international tennis team in Germany, it was the tradition to have a team party. With beer flowing all evening, each player had to sing a song from his native country. There were prizes for the best songs. I like an easy win, so I not only learned Ramazzotti's songs, but also how to imitate him perfectly, his voice, and how he moved. I took full advantage of my gift as an imitator and became really popular for this on the world tennis circuit.

Every night Takao came to my room and learned ten new words in English. Meanwhile, we communicated through tennis. We practiced together every day. I was still stronger than him, especially on clay. It was an unknown surface to him, but I sensed that this guy had exceptional qualities especially when he could master the net.

The drills were the only way we could communicate on the court. For example, playing cross-court in backspin, and then the first one who changed to the backhand, would set off the free point. He understood that I was trying to get him to use his backhand slice more and in this way to change the opponent's rhythm so that he could play variations. Indeed,

with Takao being only 5'7" tall and weighing just 165 pounds he certainly could not play power.

After a month in Holland, communication between us had already improved greatly. Takao would finally be able to understand the talk I wanted to have with him. I had been planning it for some time, and it was important. My tone was serious as I looked into his eyes. "Takao, I want to be your coach for several years, until you reach the Top ATP 100". He nodded. "I want you to be ready to travel all over the world, to compete with Europeans, Americans, South Americans, Australians, and aim for the biggest tournaments with the most ambitious programs".

Takao looked at me, taken aback by my words. "You in Japan," I continued, "are a great people, unique in the world. But you are an island and tend to isolate yourselves as a people. This is not good for someone who wants to be a professional tennis player, whose life is based on travel, and also on adaptation... Your language is spoken only in Japan, your food, which is exceptional, is the only food you are willing to eat, your medicine has been studied only for you, and your daily customs and rituals are sacred and inviolable".

"I know how much you earn when you stay most of the year in Japan and play in the Japanese championships. But Japanese national championships and tournaments, Davis Cup, Asian championships and sponsor appearances don't interest me. Except the Davis Cup... but your home must be the Grand Slam tournaments and the ATP circuit, on all surfaces and on all continents".

I could not tell from his completely impassive expression whether he had understood my speech or perhaps was frightened by it or, even worse, that he had interpreted my words as offensive to his sacred Land of the Rising Sun. But I had to take that risk. I had already realized that when you start a relationship between coach and player, you have to be totally transparent and make it clear what the shared expectations would be.

"If you want me to stop playing and become your coach, I will do so with all my heart and would hope to coach you for many years, even for your entire career" (as in fact what happened)... "but under the condition that you make a solemn commitment to step out of your comfort zone and become a 100 percent international player".

He nodded, he was very excited, and in his English he told me that he wanted to be a totally international player. He agreed to everything. We shook hands, and then bowed, in his style. The commitment was made to both the Western and Eastern modes, and he allowed no exceptions for either of us. At that moment we made the decision to embark on a beautiful path in our professional life together. This later also turned out to be a path of profound feelings, as between two brothers, yet who had been born and brought up at the two opposite poles of the earth.

The first tournament was the Japanese national championships. This was very important to him and to his sponsors. Takao at his young age was not seeded. The championships were held at the legendary Ariake tennis complex in Tokyo. Its Center Court, equipped with ten

thousand seats, was one of the most modern in the world. When it rained, a retractable roof had been built that cost five thousand dollars each time it opened or closed, just for the electricity it took.

Takao won the first round. In the second, he faced the number 2 seed, Kentaro Masuda, a strong backcourt player, very solid. Takao however defeated him in two sets. This created much surprise at the tournament. In the semifinals, Takao was clearly the underdog against his friend Satoshi Iwabuchi who was a very strong, left-handed player. Iwabuchi was very similar technically to Chilean Marcelo Ríos, who had also been World No. 1 during those same years.

Takao and Satoshi, as in Japanese cartoon stories, had grown up together, and not only because of tennis (both had been invited to the wonderful National Technical Center in Tokyo at the age of thirteen). In fact, by an incredible coincidence, they had also happened to be in the same school and class and had even been deskmates.

From the semifinals on, it was three out of five sets, which is almost another sport than two out of three. For both of them it was the first time. My very dear friend Hans Simonsson, a former Swedish champion, was Satoshi's coach. I think he was convinced that his protégé would win easily. Instead, the struggle lasted almost five hours, with Takao, giving us a glimpse of what a fighter he was, a strong point that he would display for the next fifteen years. Takao won 7-6 in the fifth, saving three match points.

The final actually came to a crescendo then, from a formal point of view. The Emperor of Japan, the "Tennō" (Akihito, the son of the historical figure Hirohito, known in his homeland as "Shōwa," and who reigned during World War II) would attend the final. As he did every year, he would be present at All Japan, Japan's national championship, to personally see who would have the honor of being awarded by him as best tennis player of the Rising Sun. The First Prize money award, in recognition of the importance of the event, was the equivalent of 100,000 U.S. dollars.

All ten thousand spectators, the Stadium's maximum capacity, had to pass through the metal detector. All had been instructed by leaflets and over the loudspeaker of the etiquette to be followed in the presence of the Emperor. For example, no one would be allowed to sit down before His Highness arrived and was seated. Another absolute rule, which all children of the Rising Sun learn at a very early age, was that in case one stood in front of the Emperor, one could not turn one's back to him. This would be a gesture that would practically be considered a national offense.

Takao was now playing in a full state of grace, and at the age of nineteen, by far the youngest player there ever, he beat Gouichi Motomura, again in five sets. His opponent had been the highest ranked Japanese tennis player before that, and an ultra-favorite for the final. Everyone was taken totally by surprise. Takao was an unknown tennis player fresh out of the Juniors stage. He was from Sapporo (in short, from the mountains) which was the capital of the island of Hokkaido (considered the ends of the earth by those from Tokyo and Osaka, that were cities on the main island of Honshu). And here was the player who had won the title. It was simply unheard of.

They brought the podium and medals to the court. Takao was stunned, not only by the excitement of having won, but also by being obliged to speak in front of all these spectators, on live national television, and before his Tennō, whom he had known only in schoolbooks. His dad, sitting next to me, wept unashamedly and repeated to me the only words he knew in English, "*Thank you, thank you,*" almost shouting to show his appreciation.

Takao had the gold medal placed around his neck. He took the microphone, and once the ritual of bowing as a sign of respect was over, he started to speak... Though from a distance, I could see that he was breathing heavily. He turned toward me, his back to the Emperor. Then, heedless of the murmur of disapproval from the audience, he began: "First, I want to thank my coach Claudio, from whom I have learned so much in these last two months, not only about tennis," and he added, just for me, in Italian, a phrase he had understood from an Eros Ramazzotti song: "Thank you for existing". I did not expect this, and as I waved him to turn around, for God's sake, toward his Emperor, I began to cry too.

Takao had just begun his speech.

"We, in Japan, are an island," he began, looking into the eyes of Tennō Akihito and Empress Michiko at his side, considered a very open-minded woman. Fortunately, I had an excellent translator beside me. "We speak only Japanese, we eat only Japanese food, and our customs are known only to us".

I couldn't believe it, he was repeating before his nation, before the near deity in the land of Japan, the most advanced country in Asia, with a culture thousands of years old, the speech I had given him privately, when I had wanted to make sure he was ready to become an international athlete. "For me this victory is just the beginning. Now I am ready, as a Japanese champion, to travel, to compete with Europeans, Americans, Australians, South Americans on courts with all surfaces, eating the food I will find anywhere in the world, and accompanied by my coach Claudio".

He continued like a raging river in front of the aghast crowd. "We have to change our mentality, and thanks to tennis I hope to be an example for all young Japanese. Travel is the university of life". Takao's father was petrified. We have to understand that a fundamental pillar of Japanese culture is hierarchy based upon roles and seniority. A nineteen-year-old boy proposing a revolution in lifestyle and Japan's world view, on TV and in front of the Tennō himself, could have triggered more than a minor scandal. I prayed, hoping that there would be no consequences.

After Takao Suzuki's speech, ten very long seconds of silence followed... The silence was broken by one man, the right one, who stood up and began to clap first. It was Akihito... The crowd followed him, reassured by the approval of their moral and spiritual leader, and produced a roar that made Takao smile, with a satisfied and knowing look, with all the innocence of a teenager. He seemed to be saying, "That's good, they've understood".

I am very fond of this story. It is one of the most beautiful and most meaningful stories life has ever offered me. I feel

that my story of Takao is an anthem against racism, a lesson for all of us that when two opposing cultures meet, in this case through tennis, both should absorb the best from one another. But this is only possible if you leave your mind and heart open.

We Had Already Called the Cab to Go to the Airport...

In the story of 'Takao Suzuki, Wimbledon 2003' there are profound lessons to be learned. They are lessons we must never forget, about how our "sixth sense," our confidence in our work, and our determination to give the most unlikely opportunities a chance, can all eventually lead to the most astounding results.

Takao was going through the worst period of his career ever. He arrived in England unwillingly for the traditional event dedicated to great tennis played on grass. This of course culminated in the most important and renowned tennis tournament in the world, Wimbledon.

The championship ("The Championships") as the British like to call their cherished tournament with a touch of smugness – as if there were no other in the world – begins with three grueling weeks leading up to the event itself.

The Wimbledon Qualifying Competition is played at Roehampton, the Bank of England's sports center, also home to the Federal Center of Great Britain and the world headquarters of the International Tennis Federation. The courts differ from those of the "The Championships", and the atmosphere is more like a picnic with strawberries. This is nothing like the austere, intimidating, and almost 'religious' atmosphere of the Church Road courts, home to Wimbledon since 1922. (Wimbledon moved to Church Road from Worple Road, Wimbledon, where it all began in 1877.)

For years now Takao and I had such a close relationship we were almost like brothers. Over the past six or seven years Takao had opened the doors of international tennis to several players from his great country. Yet now for the first time, he had strong doubts about whether to continue competing at the top level. Tennis was evolving, as it always had, and this is true of all sports. Now it seemed that champions needed power and size to attain the summits of world tennis. Takao, with his now 175 centimeters height and less than 70 kilos weight, had mistakenly convinced himself that refined technique like his was no longer enough.

We played the famous "Queen's Tournament," on grass courts that were as perfect as felt billiard tables, and lost badly in the first round. In the evening, in tears, he told me he wanted to go back to Tokyo and think over whether he should continue his pro tennis career or not. This is when the coach often becomes like a big brother and must not hesitate to shake up his protégé.

I believed in Takao more than ever and reminded him that tennis was not only about strength and size. In Japan they had created Judo, a martial art based on the technique of using the opponent's force to attack him back. This was precisely like Suzuki's game. When he played, his body was sensitive and relaxed, especially in volleying strokes, and this meant that the harder the opponent hit the ball, the happier Takao was. He was too influenced by outside factors and forgot his own true power. His was almost one of a kind on the circuit.

I convinced him to stay, even though with his poor ATP ranking he was not even eligible for a place in the qualification tournament at Wimbledon. There was, however, the preparatory tournament in Nottingham where he could at least play for qualifications. If he didn't pass, he would still have the very slight chance of maybe signing in at Wimbledon as 'Alternate'. This meant that he could get in if there were twenty players missing from the entries. I was also preciously seconded in this difficult supportive task by Mr. Muraki, a Japanese gentleman of great character and wisdom. He was the physical therapist travelling with us and went beyond the call of duty in giving moral support to both Takao and I.

In Nottingham, Takao's play began to improve, and he won the first two matches. He was then about to play the third in two days, on a Sunday. He had the options of playing in the Nottingham draw, if he won, or trying his luck as an Alternate at Wimbledon Roehampton.

He lost his match though to a local tennis player that he should have easily beaten, a certain Sherwood, like Robin Hood's Forest. Redheaded Sherwood was nevertheless a good athlete and played the best match of his life. He was not aware that he was in fact offering us a huge gift by beating Takao 7-6, 7-6.

Takao made one more attempt to leave for Tokyo without even wanting to wait a day to find out if about 20 out of 128 entrants with better classifications than his had not shown up. In actual fact, statistically he had no more than a two percent chance, but both Mr. Muraki and I kept telling him that out of professionalism and a show of good sportsmanship, for his own self-respect and to set an example for his team, he should at least try.

We waited all day. The number of missing players grew slowly, but surely. “You’re out by 12 now” I told him around two o’clock that afternoon. This meant that in three or four hours, 12 tennis players could take us out of the tournament. I didn’t have much hope anymore either. On one court, however, the last one, at No. 22, the matches were taking much longer than on the other courts. Roger Federer’s best friend, Marco Chiudinelli, won 16-14 in the third set (there was no tie-break in the last set at Wimbledon) after nearly four hours of play.

Around 6 p.m. there was only one match left to play and Takao was next in. The disappointment of not being able to play was being made even worse by such a close miss. With suitcase in hand, Takao came to say goodbye in the Club parking lot. It crossed my mind that maybe that would be the last time I would be seeing him as his coach. Unlike the joyful, enthusiastic look he usually had for everything, I could see such sadness in his eyes. I was afraid he might be on the verge of severe depression...

The cab was already approaching. Over the loudspeaker they were calling Jérôme Golmard for the second time.

He was the favorite of the qualifications tournament, a phenomenal French player. The announcement was for the last match on the last court, number 22. His opponent would be the fearsome British player, Ian Flanagan. At the Queen's tournament he had beaten Philippousis, a top Australian player and finalist at Wimbledon... "Takao, wait!" I suddenly shouted. "Golmard's not here! Go change, I'll take care of the cab". It took him just three minutes to change into his all-white kit (as is mandatory at Wimbledon). He went down to the court and overcame Flanagan with an impressive 6-2, 6-2 victory. Takao had adjusted his returns and groundstrokes instantly, without a second thought. His serves and volleys were world-class. Almost as if by some miracle, he suddenly had newfound confidence in himself and his playing.

He went to face Serbia's rising star, Janko Tipsarevic, in the second round. The match was a real struggle. Janko simply could not understand how this Japanese player with such an unimpressive ranking managed to make the most difficult of volleys and never lose his serve. Takao won the first set on tie-break. His confidence was growing exponentially and led him to break in the second set and take home the second set 6-4 as well.

We were only one match away from getting into the Wimbledon main draw for the first time. Takao's opponent was Noam Okun, an Israeli player with a powerful physique and exaggerated force in his strokes. These were precisely the two elements that three days earlier were convincing Takao to make the biggest mistake of his life, that is, to stop playing because he supposedly did not have the physical strength

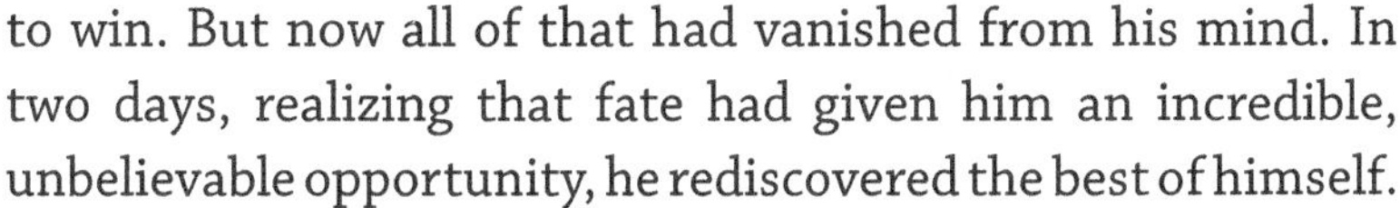

to win. But now all of that had vanished from his mind. In two days, realizing that fate had given him an incredible, unbelievable opportunity, he rediscovered the best of himself.

Okun was giving him a really hard time, and this was exacerbated by the three-out-of-five sets, instead of the two-out-of-three of the first two rounds. I watched three sets of fierce fighting. Many balls were landing near the lines, and the players were forced into Russian roulette by the woefully unprepared and superficial English line judges. They were often caught up in performance anxiety and missing the moment of the bounce, would call the ball in or out arbitrarily.

On the next court, Dick Norman was playing. He was a Belgian left-hander not only known for his height of six-foot-five and devastating serves, but also for having beaten Stefan Edberg at Wimbledon a few years before. The Swede was a tennis legend, multiple winner of Wimbledon and other Grand Slam tournaments, and had been Takao's inspiration and idol since childhood. For me, being on the bench was torture. It seemed to me a crime not to take advantage of this golden opportunity that the 'God of Tennis' had wanted to grant us. I could not stop thinking that if the cab had arrived two minutes earlier all of this would never have happened.

Takao was stronger than everyone and anything, and he overcame Okun. As he went out the court gate, journalists from Japanese TV stations armed with microphones and cameras were already elbowing to get near him. A Japanese player on "The Championships" board was the epitome for millions of tennis players of the Rising Sun.

Suzuki's match finished at the same time as Norman's. I

jokingly told Takao that I hoped the draw would put him right up against the Belgian, as proof that his technique, speed, courage, and tactical intelligence could beat the power, size, and predictability of players who responded by hitting balls at impossible speeds. Moreover, I told him that he would have a chance to avenge his idol Edberg, right at Wimbledon!

As you may have already guessed, during that enchanted week, the draw came up for the first round as precisely Suzuki and Norman, on Wimbledon's Court 17, one of the bigger outside courts. A few days passed, from the Friday to the following Tuesday, as Mr. Muraki got Takao in top physical condition. I did likewise by recreating an atmosphere of fun and enthusiasm during our training sessions. In my opinion this was the main task of a travelling coach.

On an unusually hot sunny day for June in London, Takao found himself peering up at Norman at the pre-match meeting. Norman chose to serve, a sign of confidence. Takao, with his flexibility and sharp eye, neutralized his opponent's serve that was travelling at no less than 220 kilometers per hour.

I recalled Bruce Lee's metaphor "*Be water my friend*," that expressed the need to be flexible in body and mind and prepared to adapt to any circumstance and find solutions immediately. I made up a more Japanese variation and said to Takao, "*Be tofu, my friend*". As many know, tofu is sort of the consistency of a soft vegan cheese that in Japanese cuisine is used to accompany just about everything. It perfectly rendered the idea of my advice to Takao for his match at Wimbledon.

He won in four sets. At match point I was trembling. I felt

like I was living the happy ending of a fairy tale. Takao won. The long intense hug with Mr. Muraki, in tears just like me, breaking all Japanese rules and etiquette, ended up broadcast on the Japanese NHK news.

For the records, two days later Takao challenged the Top 10 ATP player Karo Kucera. The Slovakian had a hard time winning against Takao. This was even though Takao was suffering from fever that day, perhaps from all the stress and whirlwind of such intense emotions. Now they gave way to the sheer joy of finding himself a real professional tennis player and a true star for the next ten years to come...

Thank you for existing, Takao!

At the 2008 Paris Bercy Tournament

This story begins with the big October indoor tournament that has been held since 1986 in Paris, at Bercy Stadium. I vividly remember when I made it to the qualifying round of its first edition, but because of a stupid injury I couldn't play. Indeed the night before the tournament, I had arrived at the hotel weary from travelling and was relaxing in my room before dinner. I started playing "Super Mario Land" on the Game Boy, a deadly addictive little electronic game. A good two hours passed in no time and without realizing it, I was still in the same position with my head resting on the edge of the bed's headboard.

I am still ashamed to confess that getting up, I had such an excruciating stiff neck that I was forced to withdraw from the tournament. I feel that although I have done great things in my life, when I have demonstrated courage and intelligence, sometimes quite honestly, as I think back, I also showed that I could be incredibly stupid.

It was therefore a great satisfaction for me to return to the

Bercy tournament as Simone Bolelli's coach, in his magic year of 2008. For the records, I was Simone Bolelli's coach from February 2006 to May 2009 in an exhilarating cavalcade of extraordinary results, month after month, year after year, that had taken him from being World No. 248 to No. 36. And he was No. 1 in Italy.

My interpretation of private coaching has always been based on the independent decision-making of player and coach. This concept was the cornerstone of the incredible success of the three and a half years I worked with Bolelli. The first thing we fine-tuned with Simone was goal setting and goal planning. When he was World No. 248, I asked the 19yearold youth on our first day, "Where do you want to get to?" He answered with determination, "I want to get to be World No. 1".

We were at the Forum Sporting Center in Rome. This was the home of the Academy that I had just opened with the owners of the Forum, a jewel of a sports facility, unique in Italy. Having the rooms inside the Sporting Center available gave me the great advantage of being able to train tennis players daily who were from outside of Rome, as in the case of Simone, who was from Bologna.

We arrived in Paris, and right from the first practice sessions it was immediately evident that Bolelli could be a real threat to his opponents at Bercy with the hammering of his crashing serves and forehands. And indeed, he took the first round of the tournament against a highly ranked player, a formidable athlete whom no one wanted to oppose, the

Finnish Jarkko Nieminen. Bolelli won by putting up such a fight and showing such enormous force of character at crucial points that I did not doubt for a second that he could not win the match.

The next day, October 25, 2008, he was to face the World No. 8 American, James Blake. Both Simone and I clearly saw in the pre-match that Blake would be sent home.

The Tournament granted us the canonical half-hour warm-up on the Center Court, while dividing the space among four players, as is almost always the case in indoor tournaments. Shortly before the match, news reached us that Federico Luzzi, an Italian tennis player who was a close friend of Simone's and also of mine, had died of acute leukemia. Peter Lundgren, Stan Wawrinka's coach, had come onto the court halfway through our warm-up. I was irritated because they only had the court the following half hour, and it is blatantly against etiquette to enter the court too early. We still had a good twenty minutes before the end of our practice. But then I realized that Peter was in tears.

He looked at me... "Federico is dead!" I still couldn't understand. "Federico Luzzi is dead" and he leaned on my shoulder crying. Simone saw there was something wrong. I took him aside, trying not to let him notice my shock. I told him to try two serves and then to come for a walk with me. He did them quickly, very concerned. When I told him about Federico he grew silent. I could see he was having a hard time saying a word.

An hour and a half or so later, James Blake, World No. 8,

was waiting for us on court. Though he was one of the top seeds at the Paris Bercy tournament, Simone very well knew he could beat him. The year 2008 was a magical year for us. Simone's energy level now though, compared to the previous day, was of course very different.

Simone played that very important match thinking of his friend Federico. Simone and Federico had played against each other in Como, two years earlier, and Simone had been the unexpected winner. I remember the sharp and intelligent young Federico Luzzi telling me that he had perhaps never seen an Italian player capable of accelerating his arm to such a degree as Simone at the moment of impact with the ball.

Simone, under normal conditions, would in my opinion have won that match against James Blake. He was obviously affected by the tragic news of his friend's death. He lost, after demonstrating a very high level of play for two hours.

Hong Kong 1999 and the Birth of Legal Coaching

The Salem Open...

Some twenty-five years ago a great many professional tennis tournaments were financed by the tobacco industry. I remember "Kim" and "Muratti" trophies in Italy that referred to their main tournament tobacco sponsors. Marlboro had even produced a tennis clothing line, making players look like packs of cigarettes.

I think back over my twenty years or so of air travel, often on long-haul intercontinental flights. In those days there was a "smoking section" in planes and it clearly stunk up the entire passenger cabin. The thought of those hundreds of flight hours we had to endure as we travelled to tennis tournaments around the world make me nauseous even today. Salem was the dominant industry sponsor in Hong Kong which made it possible to hold a major tournament there in April.

My long incredible coaching history with Japanese tennis player Takao Suzuki led me to hundreds of matches against top champions. In Hong Kong, it so happened that Takao was to face Richard Krajicek in the first round. Richard had been Wimbledon champion three years before. He was a friend of mine since we had played against each other when he was very young.

I was fascinated by the biomechanics of Richard's serve. In my opinion his harmony of movement was better than anyone else's at the time. He achieved maximum performance with minimum effort. Later there was Federer, who did even better in that respect. The serve is the only shot where it makes sense in tennis to talk about biomechanics, since it is obviously the only shot that does not depend on your opponent's shot. Both Suzuki and I knew it would be very hard to win that day.

Unlike any other sport, tennis had to live with an infamous "no coaching" rule for fifty years. This was ATP's regulation prohibiting (in the past, fortunately) verbal and nonverbal communication of any kind between coach and player during a match, under penalty of very heavy fines to be paid by the player. Any violation of this rule was totally at the discretion of the chair umpire. This regulation was in place even when the category "ATP Coach" did not yet exist. Nevertheless, this phantom figure apparently came to life when conditions existed, according to the referee, to fine tennis players.

The match got off to a bad start for us. Krajicek got ahead by a break, Takao recovered the break and went to serve. I was sitting slightly elevated on the short side of the court. Suzuki got up from his chair and came over, laying his towel right under me. He looked at me, I took a deep breath and returned his gaze. Takao knows how much importance we place on breathing during matches, to control heart rate and nervous tension, especially before starting an important game on a serve. Like a punch we didn't see coming, incredibly we hear the call, "*Warning, Mr. Suzuki code violation, coaching*".

In the Japanese mind, the violation of a rule is as humiliating and degrading as can be. Imagine if this is pointed out and publicly sanctioned in front of thousands of spectators. The Irish chair umpire Feltus, who is still in activity today, had interpreted my breath as advice to Takao. Fergus Murphy was therefore entitled to sanction Takao despite the obvious absurdity of a referee having virtually unlimited say.

Takao lost in two sets. After the match I went to the office of the legendary ATP supervisor Tom Barnes. I shouted that he had to put into writing to me that the resulting automatic fine to the player I coached had been for "abuse of breath". Tom, a good person with a character of gold, known for not letting himself be bullied by anyone, was clearly embarrassed. He rescinded Takao's fine on his authority, though unfortunately this would not compensate for the unjust humiliation Takao had suffered. Tom Barnes knew that I had hit the nail on the head perfectly, exposing the huge flaws in that hypocritical regulation.

That day I vowed to myself to do everything in my power at the ATP to legalize coaching, that is, the right for coach and player to communicate during official matches. But to do this, the official qualification of "ATP Coach" had to be born. Eleven years later, I ran for Coach Representative on the Players' Council, and was elected by my colleagues.

Yet it was still a long uphill struggle to the historic

achievement of banishing that tremendously deceptive regulation that forbade (in vain) coaches from communicating with players during matches.

It was unacceptable to be the target of such discrimination when compared to all other professional sports. Indeed, much more courageously (yes it must be admitted), in women's tennis, the WTA had changed this regulation many years before. According to the WTA regulation, at the end of a set, the coach was even allowed to come down to the court and talk to the player for a minute and a half.

In any case, getting around the men's tennis regulation was not difficult, and almost all the coaches had a secret code to help them, especially in difficult moments during a match. It might be added that the WTA, in allowing coaches to speak to their players during a match, had added a new attraction for TV viewers. Coaches were always equipped with microphones, and so from home everyone could hear their advice.

I began to get a taste for my new role as elected Coach Representative with the important responsibilities it entailed. Two years later I was re-elected over Patrick Mouratoglou, one of the most prominent coaches in the pro world. For my first two-year term, I had appointed Roger Federer as President and Rafael Nada as Vice President. I won the election for four terms in a row. This meant that for eight years I was to talk, discuss, explain and confront tournament directors and ATP Board Members on the subject.

Patrick Mouratoglou was involved in an incident during the U.S. Open final. The player he coached, Serena Williams, was put against the young Naomi Osaka, who was there with me. Serena was playing to break the Majors record (in tennis the four Grand Slam tournaments considered Majors are the Australian Open, Roland Garros, Wimbledon and the U.S. Open). She was the big favorite in the final against Naomi Osaka. The young Japanese player gave her a lot of trouble thanks to a phenomenal first serve.

The match was tight. Serena threw her racket to the ground in frustration because of a missed shot. The umpire called a penalty point. This was because Serena had already received a warning of which she was unaware. A few games earlier, her coach, Patrick, also caught on camera, had given Serena a nod from his box far from the court.

There was no way the phenomenal American tennis player could have noticed, given the distance. Amidst the typical din of the U.S. Open Center Court, the Arthur Ashe Court, Serena didn't even know she had received a warning. According to Serena's mental count, throwing her racket drew a first warning, not a point lost. But in actual fact it had been the second.

When the reality of the situation dawned on her, she exploded worldwide in a fit of rage mixed with despair. She blamed the umpire for making her the victim of a great injustice. She had not seen nor could she have physically felt her coach's advice. But the fault was not with the umpire. It was with that hypocritical and destructive rule in force in Slam tournaments, even in women's tournaments, that tennis had foolishly had to live with for fifty years. The facts of that day in New York in 2018 confirmed that my personal battle, that I was fortunately able to turn into a battle taken up by many

ATP members, was justified by clear and irrefutable evidence.

Meanwhile, five years before, the first step had been accomplished. I thought of Julius Caesar: *Alea iacta est*... "The die is cast". I finalized the creation of the qualification "ATP Coach" in 2013 with precise criteria to be met for a person to be included in the official list published on the ATP site. This had also been achieved with the enlightened cooperation of my colleagues, all high-profile coaches, and with the ATP staff (particularly the Tour Managers Fernando Sanchez and Konstantin Haerle). Travelling ATP Tour Managers are the pillars of the Association of Tennis Professionals. They are the link between players and tournament organizers serving much like lightning rods on an everyday basis to deter possible disagreements. Without their indispensable contribution, the Tour would simply cease to exist. Finally the day had come when we could celebrate the birth of the ATP Coach qualification. This achievement represented the fulfillment of an extremely important goal. I considered that the significance of my life dedicated to tennis had attained its greatest heights. Since that day, the most ardent ambition for any young person who decides to be a high-level coach is to obtain qualification as an ATP Coach.

From this point of view, I unquestionably contributed to writing a page in the History of Tennis, or rather, in the History of Coaching in Men's Professional Tennis. No change in regulations conceived by an ATP Coach could ever have seen the light without obtaining institutional recognition of this qualification, complete with a list of the names of these Coaches on the official ATP website. But this landmark event in the History of Coaching was only the first step towards the goal I had vowed to fulfill in Hong Kong thirteen years before...

For the next ten years, I spoke hundreds of times, via Zoom, in person, by phone and through all social networks with my fellow coaches, players (including Novak Djokovic and Andy Murray who disagreed with me), directors of top tournaments, ATP leaders, journalists, and referees. I sought their support for a new regulation that would legalize communication between coach and player during matches. This would confer upon tennis coaching the same dignity as in other sports, and put an end to coaches being "silenced," in most cases unjustifiably and absurdly.

Nevertheless, I understood the opposition of some tennis stars with the exception of Rafael Nadal. Some probably felt that this would jeopardize their advantage if the rule were changed. One of the many reasons that makes some stars almost unbeatable is also their ability to 'read' matches before others. If their opponents could have benefited from outside advice, it would have evened that advantage out somewhat.

Yet I vividly remember Andy Murray's very noble words to me when he said, "Claudio, I don't like coaching during matches, but if the majority decides that this is good for tennis, I will comply". I heard, for the umpteenth time, in his words the greatness of this tennis star. Beyond a purely tennis point of view, it was a universal human point of view that expressed the mentality and desire of stars like Murray to elevate themselves in their every word and gesture. And this is what made these stars immortal.

Ten years later, in 2022, therefore after twenty-three years, another political tennis victory for me and for the ATP leadership was achieved. This was my greatest aspiration of all, that is, to see that communication between coach and player during ATP circuit matches become legal. The ATP world circuit is now played with legal communication between player and coach during a match. The best news is that when the new regulation was implemented, no one said a thing about it. This was a sign that the new rule, which (forgive me for the self-reference) I feel very much *my own rule*, had been accepted and quietly assimilated by all, thus improving the quality of tennis.

I like to think rather mischievously that perhaps a final contribution to the adoption of the new coaching rule was made when the inimitable Roger Federer retired. He was the proudest paladin (and what a paladin) of the objectors. Yet in the men's tennis team competition (which enjoys planetary success), the Laver Cup, that Roger Federer conceived and dedicated to the great Australian champion Rod Laver, court coaching is one of the aspects that most attracts fans.

This to me is of extraordinary significance from a managerial as well as sport point of view. It improves indisputably the tennis I love by putting an end forever to the possible contamination of countless matches. Matches were weighed down for so many years with the anxiety of this rule that fortunately has now been left behind us.

A Brilliant Art Coach

Martin Simek was born in Prague to a family of nobility. His father was a poet and philosopher. His brother, Miroslav, was a theater actor who was very famous and very brave when he satirized on the stage against the Soviet regime during the Prague Spring. This was during the communist years and at his own risk, as is the case for a person under all dictatorships.

Prague was later invaded in '68 by Soviet tanks. Martin told me with tears in his eyes how his father, a few weeks before the invasion, had sensed what was going to happen in Czechoslovakia. He took 18-year-old Martin to the Prague train station and put him on a train for Copenhagen. They both knew they would probably never see each other again.

From Denmark Martin later moved to Holland, where he continued to earn a living as a tennis instructor. He learned the difficult Dutch language, and became a resident of Amsterdam. Once Martin had mastered the language, he began to contribute to newspapers and magazines as a writer and cartoonist, in addition to his tennis activity. He had an exceptional artistic vein. He continued working as tennis instructor and coach, and he was admired as an intellectual.

The days we spent together at tournaments also became opportunities for me to learn so many things from him, from how to write an article, explain a character to an audience, do an interview, and even how to perform monologues on stage. Martin had done all of these things, and I could listen spellbound to his stories forever. For example, his interview with soccer phenomenon Ruud Krol, a defender in Cruijff's fantastic Netherlands team and then captain of the Napoli just before Maradona, led me to discover how a top champion handles big matches.

Martin Simek had a particular influence on me too in that he had coached Michael Schapers, a two-meter tall Dutch tennis player with a simple, but highly effective net game. In fact, quite honestly, Martin had literally made this pupil, constructed him piece by piece, and created him. The dictionary says for the verb 'to create', "to make from nothing". In the years and decades that followed, when I became a coach myself, I always kept this very much in mind.

Michael Schapers at twenty-four went to Wimbledon, not as a tennis player, but as a spectator. He was so grateful to have managed to get tickets. He was playing locally, in Holland, and though tall and rather slow, he never came off the three meters behind the baseline. Martin thought, against all odds, that he could teach the volleying game from scratch to Michael. In fact, the young man had the quality of being very receptive and a good listener. Martin hoped that he could go on to compete in the big tournaments.

Martin received his share of sarcastic comments and snide remarks from self-made coaches, doubtful tennis journalists, and club directors who seemed to have chosen their occupations to make up for personal shortcomings and frustrations in life. Yet Martin's work was as farsighted as it was patient. He continued to explore new ways of teaching, drawing upon that special kind of creativity of the humble often seen in the '60s in Warsaw Pact countries.

And Martin worked a miracle. Thanks to him, Michael won ATP titles, broke into the World Top 30 and reached the quarter finals of the Australian Open, and even beat a certain Boris Becker. The latter was a tennis player who was destined to greatly mark my career. Taking advantage of Schapers' height, Martin taught him the fundamentals of the net game and revolutionized his serve. He also took advantage of the epochal change in tennis materials during the first half of the '80s. He provided for some of Michael's technical shortcomings with the famous Prince oversized racket.

When you consider their point of departure, with Michael a spectator at the quarter finals of a Grand Slam tournament, the work Martin accomplished and that I experienced firsthand (I lost to Michael at Roland Garros) was a true masterpiece. That was why I was convinced that I should ask Martin to be my coach, even for three hundred dollars a day, quite a sum in 1990.

Never was money better spent in my life. Although I didn't realize it, I was actually investing, not only in my improvement as a player, but above all in enriching my knowledge for my future profession as a high-level coach.

There had been talk of it for a while... The ATP was opening up new frontiers, something very exciting in the early '90s. The Association was going to organize tournaments on the world circuit. The Middle East was clearing the way for countries like the UAE and Qatar to emerge. Petrodollars seemed infinite and sports were beginning to be seen as an excellent means of promotion and enhancement in the world. And tennis, because of its characteristic universality, was the best ambassador ever.

I signed up for the 1993 Doha tournament, the first in history, and went there a week early to train. The star of the tournament was a German friend of mine who was born in 1967 like me. I had shared the rigmarole of European Junior competitions with him, from the Under-14 and Under-16, though not the Under-18 because at seventeen he had already won Wimbledon. And that wasn't the Junior tournament either, but the Wimbledon title. I'm talking about Boris Becker.

We trained there for a week, with Martin constantly reminding me to study him carefully. Maybe one day I would have the chance to beat him. I was not so convinced about that though. Boris had lots of weapons he could use to get the best of me. Not only was he a champion of an absolute level, but it was the characteristics of his playing that could give me trouble. Boris naturally got to the end of the tournament. I lost in the first round to a Russian who was making it hard on everyone, Andrej Olhovskiy. He was also a phenomenal chess player.

After Doha we were to go on to Melbourne where the Australian Open awaited me. The trip for Martin and I, which I had arranged only up to Doha (I could not know the exact day of our departure), was going to cost me more than the prize money in Melbourne. As luck would have it, while I was begging the travel agent over the phone to look for something cheaper, Boris was sitting next to me in the business center of the Marriott Hotel.

He apparently felt sorry for me, and asked if I didn't want to come on the Emir's plane with him since it had been made available as part of the deal for him to play in Doha. I couldn't believe it. Overjoyed, I told Martin, but instead it only made him angry. He took it as a gesture of pity that weakened my image before my potential opponent. I told him that it was easy to talk about pride with my money. In fact, though, I did appreciate Martin trying to toughen me up against an obvious reverential fear of Boris. If I didn't overcome my emotional weakness I would never be able to beat him. Martin though reluctantly also accepted the transportation offer.

The day before that, Martin had told me that he wanted to go to a traditional market, the souk, to buy gifts for all his friends. Everything was so cheap there. Most of the things he bought were typical Arab dress but he even got a bulky sheep mat. We tried to stuff it all into a fake Louis Vuitton suitcase ("but it seems real, who will notice, and we'll look just as good as the people who buy the real thing..."). It took about ten minutes to get the suitcase closed by finally jumping on it. Martin weighed about a hundred and twenty pounds...

On the morning of our departure, the lobby was packed with journalists and the Qatari nobility. They had come for a little farewell party for the champions who had participated in this first edition of a major ATP tournament there. Even today, it is still an important event on the calendar. The Emir's plane was waiting at the airport for departure, but one passenger was missing. It was the one who was always late, Martin, my coach. So everyone was staring at me.

When the elevator door finally opened, all eyes turned, as if already knowing something unacceptable was about to happen... It only took an instant. Martin in his haste grabbed the fake leather suitcase violently. The suitcase literally exploded right there in front of all of us. As it burst at the seams, all of Martin's personal belongings, underwear, socks, etc. went scattering over the floor of the hotel lobby.

Boris's coach, Bob Brett, threw Martin a look somewhere between hatred and disgust. Ion Tiriac, legendary tennis manager and Becker's representative, made an unflattering comment in Romanian. Martin later demanded that he apologize. I was indirectly responsible, judging by the expressions of all of these famous and important figures of the tennis world. Yet deep down, I couldn't stop laughing. I realized that I quite liked being transgressive in such a gilt and socially rigid world... I helped Martin collect his stuff in a plastic bag and we set off for the airport. Paradoxically, I was proud of him.

A youngster with rare tennis ability is exposed to conditions that force him to grow up very fast. Particularly in the 80s, without the support of Internet or smartphones, it took maturity. On the one hand, the young person under pressure was forced to develop very strong self-control. He had to be prepared to go beyond himself in front of thousands of stadium spectators and millions of TV viewers. He had to travel the world, often on his own, without the support of much more remote technology than public telephones.

To get to the top in world tennis, it took personal growth and self-confidence, not only as a tennis player, but as a youth on the threshold of adulthood. In the collective imagination, successful accomplishment of all of this was proven quantitatively by entrance into the World Top 10. Young tennis players are fragile and vulnerable when it comes to selecting the people they should trust to be close to them, or in their everyday relationships.

This also applies to family relationships, a dimension whose importance is often underestimated. From the young player's very first successes at club level, the player must deal with the understandable expectations, large and small, from his own family. That is, even when your grandmother starts asking, "So how did my grandson do today? Did he win?"

Such expectations will be the hardest obstacle to overcome for our little tennis player. Great champions also become such because even from an early age they have not let themselves be unduly affected by family expectations. Indeed, these are much more insidious than those coming from sponsors, federations, the press or managers. I was fortunate in this regard.

My family on the whole did not condition me much. However, maybe that was because as a youth I almost never lost. I was Italian Champion in the Under-14, Under-16 and Under-18 and, most importantly, World Junior Champion in 1985. In the long run, this fragility also affects the player's results on the court. Personal growth cannot be ignored if one wants to achieve truly top results in world tennis.

My "rustichella" hot sandwich at the motorway café. En route by car to the Bologna tournament we stopped at a gas station with a coffee shop on the A1 highway. We went inside and Martin saw me pay for an orange juice and the popular hot sandwich called "rustichella". I went over to the counter and asked for it. Through the glass pane we could see there was only one left, it was cold and had probably been sitting there since the day before.

Martin would not let up... he was so convinced that the way I behaved off court revealed personality problems that would heavily penalize me in matches. He turned out to be absolutely right. The man behind the counter quickly placed the untoasted moldy rustichella in a paper towel and then on a dish with my orange juice in a plastic cup. Despite being disappointed and displeased, I took the plate and, also because I was hungry, carried it to my small table, resigned to eating it.

Martin had been observing the whole scene. It all happened in a snap... "What the f--- are you doing?!" he yelled in his basic Italian. "You want to be a tennis champion and you don't even have the guts to tell this jerk to give you a hot sandwich!?" Martin was shouting at the top of his lungs. All the customers in the cafe stopped to watch. The sly proprietor realized what was happening and hurriedly went to get me a new hot ham and cheese rustichella and even brought it to my table.

Martin was more than two meters tall, with long hair and a Slavic accent. At that moment, he had the look of someone who might have killed in the past. There was war in Yugoslavia, and the proprietor didn't want to take any chances. I said nothing, but the lesson came over loud and clear. And it was also of infinite help to me in my future coaching career. Today the most important work we do is on personal growth. This is mainly by working on behavior off the court that will then be reflected in behavior on the court. You have to have the strength to fight back and claim your rights... to not accept situations out of shyness or "to keep peace". A champion faces situations and conflicts, he doesn't remain victim to them.

“Sliding Doors”

One of the most instructive films I have ever seen in my life was the 1997 film with Gwyneth Paltrow, *Sliding Doors*. The story also reflected the best explanation of how Robin Söderling chose me to be his coach. Indeed, the best things seem to happen by a margin of probability limited to the thousandths.

By March 2011, I had gained Robin’s complete trust in me on the court, as well as his esteem and friendship that were mutual, and still continue today. After the ATP tournaments in Brisbane and Rotterdam, both World Top Tournaments, Robin added a third victory, Marseille. He won against one of the most formidable players ever, a Slam winner and Wimbledon finalist, coached by the legendary Bob Brett. I’m talking about the Croatian Marin Cilic.

Between the semi-finals and finals, Robin was feeling sluggish, with a slight fever. I convinced him to have some blood tests done, and they showed nothing special. We would later remember that medical response in Marseille very well.

He went on the court, and after he lost the first tie-break 11-9, I told him that maybe it would be prudent to withdraw. He said no. He got back in the match, who knows where he found the energy, and won 6-2, 6-2.

And so, by April 2011, Robin had won every match that he had played, some 20, with the sole exception of the round of 16 in Melbourne at the Australian Open. A triumphant start to our relationship.

These back-to-back wins gave me the courage one day to ask him a question that I had felt was important. "But Robin why did you choose me last year for this coaching position? I know you were familiar with my work, even firsthand. You lost to Simone Bolelli in Monte Carlo in 2009, and I was his coach. But I was not among the coaches of a World Top 5 player".

We sat down. Robin asked me,"Do you remember in November 2009, when you came to London to the ATP Finals and we happened to cross each other with my coach at the time, Magnus Norman, in the lobby of the hotel?"

"Yes, I remember, but what does that have to do with it?" I wondered.

"Magnus asked what you were doing there in London, since you didn't have a player in the tournament. You explained that you had three days off between tournaments, and the ATP Finals were an excellent refresher course for you. You had ATP accreditation to be in the players' box and so you could watch the matches from just a few feet away. This was invaluable for you to refresh your coaching work".

I agreed about it all, yes, but I still could not see the connection...

"Well, I want my coach to have an absolute passion for tennis. A coach who has three days off at the end of the year goes... to study tennis... well, that's the right attitude for a candidate that I would want as my coach... and that's why I sought you out".

I was speechless, I had never expected an answer like that. The memory of the week I had spent just before going to London in 2009 suddenly came to mind. I was in Helsinki with Michael Berrer for a Challenger. There was generous prize money being offered and the entry list was impressive. On Monday of that week, Michael played the first round against home idol Henry Kontinen. The latter was a player who only because of injury had failed to break into the World Top 10 Singles. He was obliged to then concentrate on doubles, and he finished World No. 1.

The match was very close. With Michael and Kontinen's devastating serves, on a very fast indoor court, it was almost inevitable that they would find themselves in the tie-break of the third. The Center Court stands were jam-packed, partly because it was minus 20 degrees outside. I myself had a hard time finding a decent seat to watch the match.

The first 13 points – I repeat 13 – of the tie-break in the third were either aces or direct points with the serve. On 7-6 for Michael, Kontinen did a serve and volley, and finally Michael found the ball with a great backhand return. Henry's volley, which like all the volleys he executed, was perfect, maybe a little long, and landed a half an inch off the baseline, and everyone saw the ball was out. Michael raised his arms, I stood up and applauded loudly. The two contenders, who were good sports and also friends, went to the net for the post-match handshake. I was so happy for Michael. He had deserved a victory like this. It would truly boost his self-confidence.

"Correction! The ball was good!" It took a few seconds for everyone to realize that the voice was coming from the umpire, who curiously was still seated on the highchair. With tremendous delay, the umpire, whom I was insulting under my breath, ordered the point to be repeated.

Michael's gaze was comparable to a volcano about to erupt. Even Kontinen himself had a moment's hesitation, but then raised his fist and went to the ball boy to prepare to serve. After ten minutes of protest, to the obvious embarrassment of even the home crowd, the match went on. Kontinen's ace, and it went to seven-all. Michael was, understandably, distracted and furious by the enormous injustice done to him. His energy dropped and he lost the match.

I remember him sitting on the white couch in the players' locker room, gazing into the void without a word and shaking his head. I didn't really know what to say. When he was calmer he asked me, organized and respectful as he was, what time I wanted to book my flight to Rome the next day. We weren't going to meet again until the following Saturday in Salzburg, where the next tournament was being held (for the record, he won in the final against Finland's No. 1 Jarko Nieminen).

Now talking with Robin, my heart skipped a beat. I suddenly realized that I hadn't asked Michael to reserve a flight from Helsinki to Rome... but instead I had decided to go to London, for the ATP Finals. I was on my way, unknowingly, to that encounter with Robin Söderling who would notice my passion for coaching. And based on that meeting he offered me the most important and prestigious job opportunity of my life in men's coaching.

That late and wrong call, on a ball that had been out by half an inch, was my "sliding door"! If the ball had landed just an inch further out, even that lousy umpire would never have overruled. Michael would have gone through to the second round, he would not have played again before Wednesday, and I would never have gone to the ATP Finals in London... I would never have met Robin Söderling in the lobby of the London Marriott Hotel County Hall near the London Eye... He would never have noticed my passion and dedication to tennis, and he would never have offered me the job of coaching World No. 5.

By just one inch, my professional life had been enriched by a supreme experience. It had made me truly feel that I had achieved the goals I had set for myself when I started out, and today I am here to tell the story...

A Chat about Teaching Tennis with Brad Gilbert

This story is the most recent that I will tell in this book.

The last five or six years of my life have been dedicated to my role as Tennis Program Director (which in the U.S. is a very prestigious title) on behalf of the JTCC/Bolles in Jacksonville, Florida, that is, Junior Tennis Champions Center. The word "Champions" here standing for the opportunity to become life champions, and not necessarily tennis champions. Indeed, only a very small percentage of professionals will participate in the biggest tournaments.

My boss, the CEO of the JTCC/Bolles in Jacksonville, Florida, is Ray Benton. He is the first person in my life who, because of his charisma and humanity, I felt I could recognize as "my boss". Ray is a great American manager who was instrumental to the exponential development of our sport in the '70s and '80s. It was very exciting to learn from him that at the turn of those wonderful and unrepeatable decades, when I was a child in love with international tennis, Ray was the

Tournament Director of the "Masters," now the ATP Finals, at Madison Square Garden in New York.

On a few occasions during the year, from the time I was 7 until I turned 12, my father would let me stay up very late. One of those times was to watch TV with him when the absolute champions of tennis played each other in November each year. With the time difference, I would get up at 3 a.m. in Italy to see Ashe, Connors, Borg, McEnroe, Vilas, Gerulaitis, Gottfried, Lendl, Gene Mayer, and Wilander ... Certainly for a child, the most valuable and direct way of learning is through visual learning. That tournament contributed decisively to the growth of an irrepressible passion for tennis and for life. It led me to the decision to do anything it took to become a tennis professional.

Ray Benton was the agent for players such as Arthur Ashe, Chris Evert and Ivan Lendl (and also for a very strong basketball player of the '80s and '90s, Michael Jordan)... In addition to those almost mythic names for tennis history buffs, Ray also worked as an agent for tennis players who were not at the absolute top, but close to it.

These were players in the World Top 5 such as Brian Gottfried and Brad Gilbert. The former is one of my mentors and is also one of my former coaches (he coached me in 1992) and he was also my best man. Brad Gilbert at Madison Square Garden itself won a unique match against John McEnroe who had been considered virtually unbeatable in New York.

With one of the many leaps in time, both forward and backward that I have sprinkled throughout this book, I come to December 2022, and Brad Gilbert. He is one of the tennis personalities who most fascinated, and still fascinates, the world of professional tennis today.

Brad Gilbert was not only a Top 5 in the ATP rankings and famous for that match he had won against McEnroe. Indeed, he had driven his opponent crazy with his defensive game comparable to a spider's web. It had been replete with the extraordinary variations in direction and speed of his shots during the ATP Masters.

Brad Gilbert subsequently wrote pages of tennis coaching history with his brilliant work with Andre Agassi. Andre often refers to this in his book *Open*. He recalls the time when, in despair at how his game was regressing, he called Gilbert for help. It was the lowest point of Agassi's career, and he was suffering from deep depression. Gilbert was by Andre's side as he played Challenger tournaments, a kind of B-series of ATP tennis. It was a humiliation for Andre. It was from that point on that with Brad he pretty much started his career all over again.

He went on to win several Majors, and remained in competition until he was thirty-six. This was truly unexpected of Agassi. Much of the credit was due to Brad Gilbert. Today Brad is one of the most influential and interesting commentators and pundits on ESPN, a kind of mecca of sports in the United States. He is one of the world's foremost authorities on tennis today, particularly on coaching.

Brad is a person with a high level of communicative intelligence. He has demonstrated this with his book *Winning Ugly*, which perhaps is actually about "Winning Smart". It is a book that is popular with readers who do not necessarily follow tennis very closely. I remember a phone call from Brad. We are in regular contact thanks to Ray Benton. I often tell myself that if I have conversations about tennis with someone like Brad, it must mean that I've managed to achieve something important in my second career as coach, after my first one as player.

We talked a bit about a project I'm doing with JTCC/ Bolles in Jacksonville, Florida, on coaching in virtual reality, but very soon, of course, our conversation turned to today's fundamental aspects of coaching... Brad is certainly one of the coaches whose work has most significantly marked the history of coaching. This is notably with superstars such as Andre Agassi and Andy Roddick, the latter being another World No. 1, though who is very different from Agassi.

BRAD: The truth is there is no "one-size-fits-all" rule in tennis. At any level. Each player finds his own way, and some tools or methodologies may work for one, but certainly won't work for others...

CLAUDIO: Yes for more than twenty years now, I have expressed this every chance I get. Federations all over the world, considering themselves the custodians of an institutional way of teaching tennis, have done great damage to the sport. Over the past forty years they have tried to impose one "technique" that they call "THE Technique" on all players. Yet in fact this doesn't exist. There are as many techniques as there are players who apply them. This is easily seen at high levels of playing. It's amazing that no one realizes something so obvious.

BRAD: That's right! The key to a tennis player's improvement is how a tennis player moves on the court, in his legs, don't you think?

I take a deep breath and feel such great personal satisfaction of having read and interpreted tennis as a coach over all of these years in exactly the same way as someone like Brad Gilbert. I have been a lecturer in more than a hundred tennis coach refresher courses under various acronyms, ATP, WTA, LTA, GPTCA, USPTA and PTR (practically the whole alphabet). These are all organizations devoted to training coaches at the highest levels in the world. My two basic principles are exactly what Brad's are, and he has never even spoken to me about this before.

I tell him, "I couldn't agree with you more Brad, and you don't know what a joy it is to hear your words. This is priceless talking to you about this, and I appreciate it enormously".

He saw that we were absolutely on the same wavelength. I sensed in him a certain relief because in turn, I could bet that he, like me, has had to deal with widespread tennis ignorance – though fortunately there are numerous exceptions. Yet this is an ignorance that has pervaded the world of coach education, the world of the masters, teachers, instructors, trainers, coaches, technicians, or tennis mentors as they are known with a dozen different names...

The support of teachers, of all levels and all subjects, not only of tennis, but of areas of society as a whole, is vital. In Japan, a country that has played a fundamental role in my life, the only profession that is not obliged to bow before the

Emperor (the "Tennō," considered a demigod), is precisely the profession of teacher. Indeed teachers guarantee the future of the Rising Sun through training its young people. This awareness is very weak in our Western societies.

The lack of recognition of the value of teachers is also at the crux of the love-hate relationship I have had with my country as an adult. The country where I was born and brought up, for which I fought and had the honor of representing with the Blue Jersey. I absolutely love Italy.

The recognition of the value of a good teacher is the litmus test for assessing the degree of civilization of a country. And coaching is an art whose importance is still far from being given the recognition it deserves. In my own life history and in the history of tennis, such lack of recognition in Italy was a key reason for my decision in 2013 to go to live in another country. A country where sports culture is exponentially superior to Italy's.

I am talking about the United States of America, a country light years ahead of most of the rest of the world in this respect, and I particularly hail the state of Florida, world capital par excellence for tennis activities.